EXTENDING CREDIT & COLLECTING CASH

by Lynn Harrison

CREDITS

Editor: Beverly Manber

Layout/Design: University Graphics

Cover Design: Kathleen Gadway

Library of Congress 92-54357
ISBN-1-56052-168-6

Limits of Liability and Disclaimer of Warranty

The author and publisher have used their best efforts in preparing this book and make no warranty of any kind, expressed or implied, with regard to the instructions and suggestions contained herein. This book is not intended to render legal or accounting advice. Such advice should be obtained from competent, licensed professionals.

INTRODUCTION TO THE SERIES

This series of books is intended to inform and assist those of you who are in the beginning stages of starting a new small business venture or who are considering such an undertaking.

It is because you are confident of your abilities that you are taking this step. These books will provide additional information and support along the way.

Not every new business will succeed. The more information you have about budgeting, cash flow management, accounts receivables, marketing and employee management, the better prepared you will be for the inevitable pitfalls.

A unique feature of the Crisp Small Business & Entrepreneurship Series is the personal involvement exercises, which give you many opportunities to immediately apply the concepts presented to your own business.

In each book in the series, these exercises take the form of "Your Turn", a checklist to confirm your understanding of the concept just presented and "Ask Yourself . . .", a series of chapter-ending questions, designed to evaluate your overall understanding or commitment.

In addition, numerous case studies are included, and each book is cross-referenced to others in the series and to other publications.

BOOKS IN THE SERIES

- **Operating a Really Small Business**
  Betty M. Bivins
- **Budgeting: A Primer for Entrepreneurs**
  Terry Dickey
- **Getting a Business Loan: Your Step-By-Step Guide**
  Orlando J. Antonini
- **Nobody Gets Rich Working for Somebody Else: An Entrepreneur's Guide**
  Roger Fritz
- **Marketing Strategies for Small Business**
  Richard F. Gerson, Ph.D.
- **Financial Basics for Small Business Success**
  James O. Gill
- **Extending Credit and Collecting Cash: A Small Business Guide**
  Lynn Harrison
- **Avoiding Mistakes in Your New Business**
  David Karlson, Ph.D.
- **Buying Your First Franchise: The Least You Need to Know**
  Rebecca Luhn, Ph.D.
- **Buying a Business: Tips for the First-Time Buyer**
  Ronald J. McGregor
- **Your New Business: A Personal Plan for Success**
  Charles L. Martin, Ph.D.
- **Managing the Family Business: A Guide for Success**
  Marshall W. Northington, Ph.D.

CONTENTS

CONTENTS (continued)

INTRODUCTION

There are two kinds of people in this world: entrepreneurs and non-entrepreneurs.

The differences between the two are legion. For example, many non-entrepreneurs think that money is the root of all evil. That, of course, is nonsense. Entrepreneurs know that money is the root of all: all business longevity, all business profitability, all business stability, all business success.

Without money, even the best laid business plans lay an egg. Why? Whatever you do in business is sure to cost money. Manufacturing takes moolah. Research and Development (R&D) is a cash drain, as well as a brain drain. One frustrated practitioner defined R&D as "where you pour your money, down Rat holes and Drains." Every time you hire an employee, you have higher expenses—for salaries, benefits, payroll-FICA-unemployment taxes, workers' compensation, etc. When it comes to advertising and promotion, you get only what you pay for.

In short, money is the lubricant that helps the business world go around. And, just as money is the root of your business, a successful Credit and Collection (C&C) program is the route to money. In fact, C&C provides a tremendous business opportunity if you treat it as a tool, rather than as toil. The information in *Extending Credit & Collecting Cash* will enable you to do that—and more!

Extending Credit & Collecting Cash is not about dreary theory. Instead, its goal is to provide a practical C&C guide for the emerging entrepreneur.

In Chapter 1, you will discover how important a go-for-it attitude is to Credit and Collections success. As one C&C manager puts it, "Credit and Collections is a lot like bungee diving. You may have all the equipment—the forms, the data, the analyses—you need to succeed, but if you don't have the heart to jump off the platform, you won't get anywhere!"

In Chapter 2, you will see how the business environments—both internal and external—can endorse, inhibit, incapacitate or otherwise influence your eventual C&C success. You will find that you can use your knowledge of the business environment to support and exhort, rather than abort, your program's effectiveness.

In Chapter 3, you will see how you can use credit terms, specifically payment criteria and reasonable account limits, to facilitate sales and promote timely payments.

In Chapter 4, you will get the line-by-line specifics you need to design an effective credit application form—one that helps you collect the right information from the right people, at the right time, in the right way.

In Chapter 5, you will learn how to analyze and leverage the general, financial and reference information you receive via credit application forms. It is relatively easy to separate legitimate firms from the confirmed frauds, to tell the creditworthy from creditworthless.

In Chapter 6, you will get the information necessary to design your billing and internal Accounts Receivable control system. Here is where it all comes together—or all falls apart. The quantity and quality of the work you did vis-a-vis Chapters 1 through 5 will determine whether your system sails or fails.

In Chapter 7, you will learn the secrets to successful collections—the attitudes, strategies, options and techniques necessary to optimize your profits and minimize costs.

There is no denying that C&C holds an important place in any entrepreneurial enterprise. So put a good program into place in your business. It will insert big profits on your Profits & Loss.

CHAPTER ONE

THE RIGHT ATTITUDE

THREE TRUTHS OF C&C

Credit and Collection systems are to the entrepreneurial enterprise what bladders are to the human body—not the most pleasant of subjects, but necessary to a clean and effective operation.

Actually, the C&C subject itself is not a problem. The real difficulty—C&C's definitive dilemma—is the illogical fears and foibles that C&C is often subjected to.

Most beginning businesspeople approach C&C with the same trepidation one usually reserves for IRS agents, dentists and in-laws. Why? They are afraid that tough collection policies will alienate customers and annihilate sales. They are embarrassed when they have to follow up a sales call with a collection call. They believe that when you confront a customer, you also affront a customer.

This counterproductive attitude counteracts common sense. The first step in developing a sound C&C system is to forget your fears and develop a shrewd attitude. Recognize and accept the following Truths and you will be on your way to developing a profitable program.

TRUTH #1—Virtually every business extends credit.

What is credit? Credit is both a function of timing and payment instruments. When a customer pays with something other than cold, hard cash, what you have is a credit sale. When a customer pays after your product or service is delivered, you have a credit sale.

What does this mean? It means that when you accept a payment by check, you have extended credit to the customer. As anyone who has ever taken a bad check will tell you, cash and checks are *not* the same thing. When you accept a check, you are crediting the customer with having sufficient funds in the bank to cover it.

If you deliver your product or service before receiving payment, you are extending credit. Many business people do not interpret payment terms (e.g., 2/10 net 30) as a form of credit, but that is exactly what they are. Again, you are crediting your customer with having the willingness and ability to meet your payment parameters.

Defined in this way, credit looks less like a *calculated risk* and more like a *standard operating procedure*—which is exactly what it is.

TRUTH #2—C&C is not a *necessary evil.* It is a business opportunity.

Credit creates opportunities for both you and your customers. Consider both sides of the credit equation.

Customers like credit. Even if they do not want to use it, they want to feel like it is there for the taking—and the taking advantage of. Vendor credit allows buyers to leverage their efforts and their purchasing power. They use it for the following reasons:

- Credit is convenient. Paying bills in cash is a monumental, and fundamental, pain. It is easier to pay one bill per month than it is to pay cash every time you need something. And, carrying cash can be dangerous, as well as a distraction.
- They may not have sufficient cash. It is a simple premise: customers do not have the money now, but they want and need to buy the product now. Given the choice, most customers would rather *pay* with credit than postpone product purchases.
- No other credit is available. Translation: no bank, venture capitalist, relative, etc., will lend your customer the money he needs to buy your product. So, if you want a sale, *you* have to lend it to him. In other words, you are the customer's *lender of last resort.*
- It creates captive creditors. Many customers buy on credit because it gives them a hold on their vendors ("I'm not paying my bill until you . . ."). They believe, correctly, that credit leads to more vendor commitment, better service, faster problem resolution, etc.

- It facilitates expansion. Growing businesses often have cash flow problems. Vendor credit can help them bridge their Accounts Receivable-to-Cash gap.
- It eases accounts payable management. If a customer can pay $1,000 now or pay $1,000 in 45 days, he might as well take his time. There is no profit in promptness.
- It creates a paper trail. Cash purchases are notoriously hard to document. Accounts Payable records, however, document every important who (who ordered the product), what (what was purchased), when (purchase date), where (delivery site), why (why the bill totaled *X* dollars), and how (how the bill was paid—as a lump sum, in installments, sans discount or finance charges). A credit *paper trail* makes it easy to track both corporate purchases and purchasors.
- It strokes their ego. Offering credit, more than anything else, is a vendor's way of demonstrating faith in a customer. Money talks, but credit yells.

Conversely, successful sellers love to extend credit because it helps them:

- Provide a valuable, and highly valued, customer service. Again, customers want access to credit, whether or not they use it. Isn't *giving customers what they want* what business is all about?
- Create sale. Many—most—companies and public organizations cannot pay cash. *Cash-n-carry* goes outside their business and bureaucratic bylines. But they can and will pay—with credit. Without credit, you would lose their business.

  A sound C&C policy can increase sales by controlling sales. For example, employee theft is a major concern to every small business. You do not have enough manpower, or enough power over men, to stop all stealing. However, selling goods and services on credit can lessen internal security problems by minimizing cash on hand and creating the all-important paper trail.

NOTE: You can use other tactics to facilitate honesty. For example, merchants started *odd-pricing* their goods—charging 99 cents for a product rather than $1—because clerks were pocketing the bills. Forcing employees to make change also forces them to access the cash register.

- It increases profits at the margin. Economists call this concept *economies of scale.* Generally speaking, the more units of an item you produce or sell, the lower your per-unit cost. Therefore, when credit increases your aggregate business, it simultaneously increases your profit-per-unit. Credit, in this respect, almost pays for itself.
- It allows you to reach a broader spectrum of customers. Cash-only payment policies often freeze out both ends of the business spectrum. Large bureaucratic organizations will not pay cash. Small, cash-poor companies cannot pay cash. Credit allows you to expand your customer base.
- You get higher returns. Customers expect to pay for credit. They typically pay in the form of lost discounts, interest charges, higher product prices (cash-only companies are often discounters), minimum order lots, and so on. Their loss—cost—is your gain—income.
- You can obtain and strengthen your customer loyalty. Credit demonstrates your loyalty to, and faith in, your customers. Long term credit implies a long term commitment. Loyalty is a two way street—you give it and you will get it back. When you obtain loyalty, you retain customers.
- You can compete successfully. A strong credit program is a good marketing and sales tool. Credit is easier for customers to analyze and evaluate than intangibles such as product, value, quality or customer service.
- It helps you document your company's track record. If you want to secure bank financing, you need to demonstrate a sound and secure business infrastructure. As any banker will tell you, viable businesses require a viable credit program. The only exceptions are small retailers or cash discounters.

- It promotes a positive and profitable company image. The relevant issue is not "Can I afford to offer credit?" It is "Can I afford *not* to?" Odds are, you cannot afford to have your business look less successful or less receptive to customer needs than your competitors. This is particularly true for those beginning businesses that are long on image and potential, and short on everything else.

To make a long story short, credit facilitates, rather than debilitates, your business. And, *what is equally important, it does the same for your customers.* Credit creates a win-win situation where everybody can score big profits.

As a result, you should focus on what credit will do *for* you, rather than what it could do *to* you.

Your Turn

List opportunities that Credit and Collections has given you, both as a customer and as a vendor.

- Would these opportunities have been as great if credit had not been available?
- Where would you be now without access to credit?

TRUTH #3—The C&C subject is no more subjective than other business basics.

Few beginning businesspeople treat Credit and Collections—particularly the *Collections* component—with any semblance of sanity. They act as though it were an infection in the business. It frightens them, embarrasses them, distresses them, intimidates them.

It should not.

If you were in this position, what would frighten you about collecting your past dues? Would you be afraid you might lose a customer? Remember, if a "customer" does not pay his bills, he is not a customer, but a charity case. Furthermore, if you cannot discuss touchy subjects with your customers, you have a pithy problem that extends far beyond your C&C system.

Why would you be embarrassed at having to collect what is rightfully yours? If you have to actively collect from a customer, it is because he did not pay his bill. *He broke the financial faith—the credit contract—not you.* He is the problem. You cannot shoulder the embarrassment for other people's failings. The bottom line is that when a customer owes you money, the money in question is *your money*. You have a right to know what has happened to it.

Why should you be distressed? Because you will not collect every account? Because sometimes, occasionally, your collection efforts will *fail*? Viewing C&C in the right light will help you lighten up. For example:

1. Accept the fact that you will not, and cannot, collect every account. That is *not* the goal of a profitable C&C plan. If you collect on every invoice, your credit policies are too strict; you are turning away acceptable accounts. There is no profit without a calculated, and sometimes misjudged, risk.
2. Do not think of uncollected accounts as horrendous mistakes. Learn from them, and think of them as a cost of doing business.
3. When analyzing your C&C program, think in terms of aggregate profits, rather than separate accounts. You care about total profits ("We made $10,000 on the lot of them!"), not single account totals ("Gee, we lost $20 on the Crittendon Account!"). It is important to see the forest for the trees.

Why would you be intimidated? C&C is not short for "Challenge and Confront" or "Cry and Cajole." C&C is a function of "Communication and Cooperation." It means letting a customer know when he or she is not meeting your expectations and his or her own contractual commitments. It means working with customers to insure that they can cover their payment promises. It means getting paid for what you do and what you sell. It means *business*.

If you run your C&C department under the same objective business principles you practice in your other departments, you will run into unqualified success.

For example:

- Communicate with your customers. Be open and up-front. Tell them, for example, "We note that payment was due on this account last month. Until this account balance is cleared, we cannot process any further purchases."
- Use teamwork. Generate C&C support from all employees—salespeople, customer service reps, etc. Make sure, for example, that all salespeople understand and accept your need for audited financial statements. They may have to explain to their customers why these reports must accompany initial credit applications.
- Keep an eye out for potential problems and nip them in the bud (e.g., make your first collection contact when an account is a month, rather than a quarter, overdue). Do not wait until it is too late.

MAKING IT WORK

The proprietor of a mid-sized lumberyard puts it this way: "The average businessperson doesn't appear to have a lot in common with Mohammed Ali. Ali used to float like a butterfly and sting like a bee; businesspeople have always floated checks and gotten stung by bank charges. As they say, 'That's life!'

"Ironically, in real life boxers and businesspeople have much in common. Like boxers, the more contact we have with others, the more likely we are to win the Credit and Collections match.

"I consider Credit and Collections a contact sport, because a successful system is built on CONTACTS. Unfortunately, we often forget to contact the people within our own businesses; we forget to support, stregthen and sell the system.

"Entrepreneurs should do what they can to punch up their internal systems prior to collection problems. It makes good business sense. Employees with the right C&C attitude can more easily strike a responsible chord with debtors.

How do you supportively hit home? Well, your best right hook is a *write* hook!"

Review the following memos. Memos like these help create the proper Credit and Collections atmospheric ambiance.

SAMPLE SALES JOB—C&C STAFFERS

If your Credit and Collections staff does not actively collect on your accounts, your accounts will passively collect dust. That's why you need a memo like this one—to motivate your manpower.

MEMO TO: Jane Dough, Credit and Collections

MEMO FROM: John Smith, President

Jane, did you know that you're a VIP? Well, you are. You are Very Important to Profits. You are closer than anyone to the asset—Accounts Receivable—that will soon be cash. Salespeople make the sales, but YOUR actions are what make the money. After all, if we don't collect the money we haven't made a sale. We've made an "involuntary donation."

I know you have a lonely assignment. It's natural for sales reps to think of themselves as "customer support" and your function as "customer abort." Further, I know that you often find yourself in the middle of a "damned if you do, damned if you don't" dilemma. We want you to be tough on bad debts, but easy on the debtors.

You have a tough task, and I want you to know that we appreciate how you tough it out. If you find that my attitude or actions debilitate—rather than facilitate—your efforts, please let me know.

I want you to know that your work—like the way you collected that $8,525 from Anderson's last month!—is more than just appreciated. You and your work are vital to our corporate success.

SAMPLE SALES JOB—SALES STAFF

The successful Credit and Collections department is seen as a valuable team player, not as a team slayer. On a regular basis, you should remind the "natural enemies" of your Credit and Collections department just how vital and valuable it is. A short memo like this one is all it takes:

> MEMO TO: Frank Jones, Sales Department
>
> MEMO FROM: John Smith, President
>
> We've all been there: we finally land "the big one" and *then* we find out that we have a big problem. The Credit and Collections department won't give "the big one" credit. End result: even though the prospect swallowed your sales presentation hook, line, and sinker . . . he's still "the one that got away."
>
> It's only human to want to blame our Credit and Collections department for your disappointment. Human, but inhumane.
>
> Next time you're tempted to fault our Credit and Collections department, please consider this:
>
> Credit and Collections is perhaps our most critical—and probably our most criticized—customer service. It is also our most powerful sales support service. Without credit, most of your customers could never have given you their first order. Without collections, none of them would have been able to give you their second.
>
> Our Credit and Collections people have to do a lot of customer service "dirty work." They make it possible for us to clean up, profit-wise. Please give them the respect and consideration they deserve.

SUMMARY

Credit and Collections is unquestionably a self-fulfilling prophecy. If you expect trouble, you will get it. Even worse, you will *create* it. On the other hand, if you expect things to go smoothly, your system will help you make a pool of money.

In all C&C scenarios, *attitude is everything!* Worrying about Credit and Collections—or worse, avoiding it—generates problems and degenerates your entire business structure.

Maintaining the proper attitude—treating C&C as a basic, nonthreatening business function—can increase your intestinal fortitude and help you stomach even the most frustrating credit conditions.

It is food for thought. Success feeds on Credit and Collections.

ASK YOURSELF

Analyze *your* attitude toward Credit and Collections. Is it positive, active, responsible, mature? Or is it *typical?*

- Do you openly discuss C&C at your management meetings, or is the subject subjected to consensual silence?
- Do you have formal (e.g., written) C&C policies and procedures? Analyze and formalize all C&C issues to insure continuity, efficiency and quality control.
- Is your C&C function handled by a lower level, jack-of-all-trades type employee (e.g., the only person too low to delegate it away)? Is this the way you typically treat crucial business functions?
- If you advertised in your local newspaper to fill the above referenced position, would you specifically mention Credit and Collections? Or is the applicant's ability and willingness to generate cash flow less important than his or her ability to type fifty-five words per minute?
- Does your C&C staffer have formal Credit and Collections training? Informal training? Such training, while not directly C&C related, can help him or her do the job. Examples include seminars on improved written or verbal communications, and stress management and personal motivation. Is he or she familiar with collection practices and legal limitations?
- Are Credit & Collection functions listed in your job descriptions as "other duties as assigned," "miscellaneous" or "other"? More importantly, is C&C *treated* as though it is of secondary importance? Does some variation of this sound familiar? "Mike, after you have typed these letters, filed these reports and made the coffee, try to make a few collection calls."
- Do you treat the person who handles your C&C like he or she is a second class citizen?

- Why is it a mistake to focus on collecting *every account*?
  - Is your C&C staffer your lowest paid employee?
  - Is his office at the periphery of your property or in the "closet office"?
  - Does he or she have the fewest or lowest quality resources?
  - Do other staffers ask in a friendly, personal way about his or her daily progress? Is he or she your proprietary pariah?

Over the last six months, what percentage of your sales, both in terms of dollar values and number of transactions, involved:

- Checks
- Standard payment terms (e.g., 2/10 net 30)
- Installment plans

What percentage of these sales—again, in terms of dollar values and number of transactions—generated collection problems? Compare the *overall percentages* to the *problem percentages*. Are your C&C fears out of proportion, given the wide disparity between *credit used* and *credit abused*? Are you letting your emotions, rather than the facts, control your attitude?

How can the reasons that buyers want access to vendor credit be used to leverage your sales presentations? In what specific ways can you use this credit opportunity to your distinct advantage?

How can the reasons that most vendors extend some form of credit to their customers be used to facilitate other internal or external business functions (i.e., sales, marketing, advertising, financial forecasting)? In what specific ways can you use this credit opportunity to your businesses' advantage?

CHAPTER
TWO

RESEARCHING THE CREDIT & COLLECTIONS ENVIRONMENT

THE BUSINESS ENVIRON-MENT

No man, and no man's business, is an island unto itself. Both must exist within their competitive environments, and respond to and consider a variety of conditions—economic, social, competitive, technological, etc. This means creating and crafting specific departments and procedures to capitalize on, or negate, the effects of the business' surroundings and influences.

It is critical to C&C sufficiency that you have a solid understanding of the business environment. The road that leads to a successful C&C program is rocky and filled with problems. Even the experienced businessperson is bound to have problems. Here is why.

Two basic issues drive the C&C program:

- The kind of program you offer
- The criteria a customer must meet to receive credit

These issues can drive you crazy. Why? Because you cannot simply map out the C&C route you want to take, and then put your business plan on autopilot. Changes in your business environment—for example, fluctuations in the local economy or an improved competitive position—can detour even the best plan.

The bottom line is you do not drive your C&C program. At best, you are part of an enormous steering committee.

FOUR ENVIRONMENTAL INFLUENCES

Four environmental influences—you might think of them as back*seat drivers*—will greatly affect what credit you offer and who you offer it to. These influences are:

1. Economic conditions
2. Your industry and competitors
3. Your customers
4. Internal issues

You need to research and continuously track these influences. You need to know how they can and will effect your business, and how your C&C program could and should inflate—or if necessary, mitigate—their impact. You must stay informed so that your C&C program can, if necessary, be reformed. This is how you insure that your program will be both realistic and idealistic.

You will need to constantly review, analyze and modify your existing program. Common timetables for reassessment are quarterly, semiannually, annually, biannually or whenever there are substantial changes in:

- Local unemployment figures—particularly if you run a retail business
- Economic conditions—recession, depression, expansion, local growth or contraction in your customer base, etc.
- Competitors' C&C policies
- Competitors' non-C&C packages—can your C&C policy help reduce a competitor's gain from new products, lower prices, better warranties, etc.?
- Your profitability
- Your cash flow
- Your total bad debt
- Average age of your outstanding debts
- Your sales figures—is your credit policy too restrictive, choking off sales?
- Number of internal complaints about your program
- Number of external complaints about your program
- C&C staff turnover

In short, you need a business that is a part *of* its environment—not apart *from* its environment. The *ofs* thrive; the *froms* do not survive.

We will discuss these influences one at a time.

ENVIRONMENTAL INFLUENCE #1—ECONOMIC CONDITIONS

As an entrepreneur, you do not control the national or local economy. The best you can do is go with the cash flow, to control your own C&C program so that it addresses current economic realities.

This is relatively simple: negative economic conditions, local or national, can impact your customers' ability to pay their debts and your ability to absorb losses. Conversely, positive economic conditions, local or national, can decrease credit risks and make it possible for you to expand or liberalize your program.

That is why you have to be sensitive to economic ebbs and cash flows.

Consider your local economy. Local layoffs can empty your emporium and your cash register. For example, the Colossal Corporation, an international manufacturer, announces it is closing its local factory. As an operator of a popular downtown stationery store, you and your business have a lot to lose. In terms of the future, you would lose:

- The Colossal Corporation's business
- Retail customers (e.g., the former employees of the Colossal Corporation would leave the town)
- Business from the small service and retail shops that were supported by Colossal Corporation and are now thwarted by a lack of business. These include businesses such as florists, delivery services and cafeteria operators.
- Additional retail customers—the former employees of the small service and retail shops who are now, due to their economic losses, former customers.

You would probably lose something on your current and past due business and personal accounts. You would have to write off some bad debts, as your tripped-up customers tried to get back on their financial feet. If they could not right themselves, you would be left holding the bad-debt bag.

In short, if the Colossal Company closes up shop, it would create a colossal calamity, a domino dilemma. Your business would spiral down in a vicious circle. You would be a victim of proprietary proximity of a languishing locale.

National negatives or political positives can have an impressive impact, too. Imagine a crippling credit crunch, one that hobbles large and small businesses. Your most important vendors would not be able to secure financing from their banks; they would turn to you for credit. You would have to answer some tough questions:

- Can I turn up my credit volume without reducing my profits?
- Will I have to turn away some customers and their profitable purchases?
- Will I be forced to offer more credit to fewer customers?
- Do my customers—based on their past payment history, financial footing, credit references, importance to my business, etc.—deserve a larger credit line?
- What will happen if I do not give them additional credit?

We can approach this credit tangle from a different angle. What would happen if Larry Lendshark, the Loan Officer down at the First Trashional Bank, erased your line of credit? Could you continue to float customer financing? Would you need to tighten or shorten your payment terms? How would you do this? Would you have to replace *free financing* with *pre-payments*? Is your picture realistic or idealistic?

Keep tabs on your local and national economic conditions so that you can guarantee a Credit and Collections program that considers these critical issues. (You might think of your program as an *economic impact statement*). This will allow you to make changes in your C&C program before you lose much more than pocket change. A successful C&C program changes with the times and the economy.

ENVIRONMENTAL INFLUENCE #2—YOUR INDUSTRY AND COMPETITORS

In some industries, credit plays a vital, center-stage role. In others, it is no more than a bit player—two bits here, six bits there. But as they say in show business, there is no such thing as a small part, only small actors.

The same premise applies to your C&C program. You can offer a lot, or a lot less. Whatever you decide to provide, your Credit and Collections program will play an important role in defining your corporate character.

There is only one problem—your C&C role will be played out among a *cast of thousands*. Your firm's development will be greatly influenced by those characters who call themselves your *competitors*. Standard industry practices, for example, will provide important parameters or guidelines for your specific credit policies. So will the individual program planks offered by other organizations.

Your decision to offer more or less or the same credit as your competitors poses a dilemma:

- You lose a potential competitive advantage if your C&C system is similar to your competitors'.
- All things being equal, you cannot afford to offer your customers less than your competitors do.
- Even marginal improvements over standard industry terms can hurt your profit margin—even as they improve your sales!

What To Do About the Competition

What can an entrepreneur do? *First,* recognize the important competitive role that a Credit and Collections program can play. *Second,* recognize that you cannot make C&C decisions in a self-centered stupor. These decisions are made in an inherently hostile territory, in a competitive, make-money-or-you-won't-make-it atmosphere. You do not operate your business in a vacuum—you must cooperate with competitive pressures.

For example, imagine you sell a top-quality product at a fairly good price. Unfortunately, potential customers see your wondrous widget as a commonplace commodity, one they could buy easily from your competitors. Marketing your widgets via product differentiation appears impossible.

It would come as no surprise if your competitors decided to compete via credit differentiation. Since price, quality and customer service are not everything, credit and payment terms can be influential in potential customers' buying decisions. Therefore, your competitors offer an array of credit arrangements, including:

- Competitor A offers payment terms of 2/10 net 30. The total amount is due in no more than 30 days; if the customer pays his bill in full within 10 days, he is allowed a 2 percent discount. This discount rate translates to an equivalent of 36 percent per year (see Chapter 3). If a buyer can get financing at less than 36 percent interest, he is money ahead to borrow from somebody else, "borrow" that money from sums set aside to pay his other bills, and pay A immediately.
- Competitor B offers payment terms of net 60; it offers no C.O.D. or fast pay discount. B charges interest at 10 percent per annum on all accounts over 61 days old. In essence, B's customers get a free 60 day loan.
- Competitor C offers a 5 percent C.O.D. or *pre-pay* discount. That is a tremendous price break on what vendors view as a *commodity*—almost enough to break his competitors' business backs.

The ugly truth: your product may be better than your competitors'. However, if your customers do not see any difference, they will base their purchasing decisions on something other than the product. If you do not offer competitive or better credit terms than your competitors, you may lose business to competitors.

Third, research the C&C programs offered in your industry and by your competitors. The more you know about them, the easier it will be to develop your own competitive plan.

When researching other plans, collect all of the written C&C related information that you can. This will include credit application forms, sales brochures, sales proposals, etc. You want to determine:

- Standard credit terms for your industry (e.g., fast pay discounts, pre-pay discounts, net payment dates, interest and finance charges)
- Credit terms offered by specific competitors
- Criteria customers generally must meet to qualify for credit—depending on your industry, this could include credit reports, personal and professional references, financial ratios, collateral, personal guarantees, years in business, etc.
- How well standard terms have worked in your industry
- The success of your competitors' credit programs
- Modifications you could make to standard industry terms that would work in your business' favor (e.g., a higher discount rate, longer discount qualification deadlines, longer net payment date, higher or lower interest charges, etc.)
- Modifications you could make to a competitor's C&C program that would work favorably in your business

Where to Get Your Information

Researching industry and/or competitor credit programs is relatively easy; it is also time-consuming, given that credit programs change with the times. You need a well organized research effort to minimize your time investment. Your best bet is to get information from:

Your vendors—specialty vendors, in particular, will be aware of what others in your industry are doing.

Your customers—they will let you know if and when your competitors offer a better deal.

Industry non-competitors—people with businesses similar to yours who, due to their locations, are not competitors.

Banks and factors—they tend to keep close tabs on their clients' C&C programs.

Relevant professional organizations—to locate appropriate industry groups, check Gale's *Encyclopedia of Associations* at your public library.

Credit organizations—chief among these is the National Association of Credit Managers, which operates as an international, national and regional resource.

Credit reporting companies—such as Dun and Bradstreet.

Relevant professional publications—to find magazines specific to your industry, check your public library for Ulrich's *Guide to Periodical Literature,* which lists over 40,000 international periodicals.

Getting inside C&C information is like getting a "Peeping Tom" perusal of your competitors' business plans. It puts you in a position of power. You can decide to play the game their way and can choose to use similar credit policies. Or, you can decide to make your own rules, policies and procedures that enhance your individual competitiveness and corporate image. You can decide to institute tighter credit policies, and keep your profit margins high and your risks low.

Whatever strategy you select, if you know the other guys' game plans, you come from a position of strength. You can play to win.

It is critical that you investigate your competitor's C&C programs with the same diligence you use when you investigate their products, prices, etc. C&C is not the least of their offerings—it is as important as any of the others.

ENVIRONMENTAL INFLUENCE #3—CUSTOMERS

The customer credit environment always operates within a *give and take* framework. You give credit; your customers take it.

Ideally, however, you will also create a *take and give* environment; that is, you will create an environment where you enthusiastically take any C&C suggestions your customers are willing to give. This feedback function is vital to a successful Credit and Collections program. Only your customers can tell you if you are offering more than they want, or less than they need. If you offer more or less, what you have is not customer service; it is self-serving.

Ask for Feedback

Sound your customers out. Ask them how they feel about Credit and Collections and, more specifically, how they feel about your current program. Be direct. Discuss:

- Specific customer needs
- Specific customer wants
- Acceptable C&C tradeoffs
- How specific C&C policies affect customer behavior

Needs, wants, tradeoffs and buyer behavior can be tricky to track. Take customer needs, for example. Some customers, such as local or national government bodies, do not need credit. At least, not in the traditional *risk-taking* sense. What they need is time—time to process the purchase-through-payment paperwork. If you give them the time they need, they will give you the business you want. When it comes to dealing with governments, *time, not credit, is money.* You will make money if you do not try to make haste.

Fulfilling customers' wants can be particularly profitable. Customers prefer Credit and Collection policies that complement their own proprietary patterns. For example:

- Underfinanced, under-pressure purchasers are probably in the market for installment pay plans.
- Cash-cushioned corporations will want to pad their profits via fast pay or C.O.D. discounts.
- Long net payment dates will facilitate proprietors who purchase supposedly *self-liquidating* products.
- Most small companies like to receive bills after they send out their own.

Once you determine what your customers want, consider providing it. It is not that big a stretch. After all, you do it with products and services. Do it with your C&C policies and you will do well.

Customer *Give and Take*

There are, of course, tradeoffs inherent in any C&C setup. Ask any customer what he needs and wants out of your program and he will tell you: everything—fast pay discounts, free financing, partial pay options, high credit limits, etc. Go beyond the superficial needs and wants to determine what your buyers really want and need—and how much they are willing to pay for it. For example:

- Are customers willing to pay higher product prices in return for your *free financing*?
- Will your customers give personal account guarantees in return for high-as-the-sky credit limits?
- Will your customers sign credit contracts vis-a-vis their partial payments?

There is no such thing as a free lunch. There is, however, a *fee lunch*. Ask your customers what they are willing to pay for their needs and wants, and then give them what they pay for. Of course, the price of your product should reflect any C&C overhead.

Finally, in the C&C *give and take,* do not give more in concessions than you expect to receive as a result of them. Credit and Collection policies, particularly those concerning concessions, should be designed to maximize your customers' bill-paying behavior and minimize your loss. In short, you need to balance a C&C policy's cost and its benefits. Here are some examples:

- If you currently offer payment terms of *net 30* and all of your customers pay within 10 days, it does not make economic sense to institute new 20/10 discount terms. You will lose 2 percent off the top without netting any gains.

  If your competitors have recently instituted a fast pay discount, that may be another story, with a less happy ending.
- If non-discount, C.O.D. payment terms are standard practice in your industry, do not offer a C.O.D. discount unless the discount serves a cost effective sales marketing function. You will experience profit margin pain with no corresponding gain.

Customer behavior is about as easy to predict as the weather. Relatively benign C&C restrictions can generate a storm of protest from customers. Tighten or discontinue discounts and you may end up with a flood of negative feedback. Loosen your credit criteria and conditions and your current customers may be thunderstruck. Typical customer responses include: "Am I subsidizing your *no-account* accounts?" To state a cliche, every silver lining has a cloud.

Before you change your C&C policies, make sure they will change customer payment behavior positively—that is, for the good of your bottom line. Remember that your C&C program should be geared toward serving customers. The more you know about their credit needs and practices, the more likely you are to devise a wise credit plan.

ENVIRONMENTAL INFLUENCE #4—INTERNAL ISSUES

Your Credit and Collections program is a function of both *influences*—your individual perspective, personality, priorities and paradigms—and *out-fluences*—those outside environmental factors already mentioned. The smaller your business, and the larger your role in it, the bigger these *influences* will loom. After all, C&C is more than an objective *function*. For most entrepreneurs, it also generates a *disfunctional fear.*

Clearly, C&C is a subject that influences virtually every component of your business. For example, your Credit and Collections collage can speed or impede your:

- Business goals
- Sales
- Marketing
- Advertising
- Financing
- Staffing needs

As a result, you must deal with what C&C means to you and your business. Again, you need to ask yourself some tough questions and tough out the answers. For starters:

How secure am I—both financially and emotionally?

How secure is my business?

Credit insurance can help allay fears and defray losses. A few caveats:

- Make sure your policy covers everything you want covered (e.g., do special policy provisions or riders exempt your most risky business?)
- Make sure your policy covers only what you want covered (e.g., insurance premiums are usually set as a percentage of sales. Make sure you are not paying a percentage on sales to cash customers, C.O.D. accounts, governmental bodies, public utilities, etc.)
- Investigate your co-insurance options (e.g, does it make the most economic sense to insure your accounts at 75, 80 or 90 percent of their cash value?)

  NOTE: No credit insurer covers accounts at 100 percent of their face value. If your accounts were 100 percent insured, you would have no incentive to turn down clients—even those with rotten credit records.
- Check all policy dates *very carefully* (e.g, *back coverage policies* and *forward coverage policies* have different deadlines. You will cancel critical coverage if you accept the wrong timeframe.)
- Check all policy definitions *very carefully* to be sure you are covered under the important ones (e.g., the big insurers have a baker's dozen definitions for the term insolvent.

Your Turn

Answer the following:

- How secure is my financing?
- Do I have a cash cushion?
- How risk adverse am I?
- What do I need to give?

- What do I want to give?
- Are my answers to the three previous questions acceptable to me, given my profit margin?

Two Special Issues

Two internal issues merit particular attention: your C&C track record, including past practices and present realities, and non-C&C corporate conditions. If you can get a handle on these concerns, you will be handling things very well.

1. Past practices and present experience

Most entrepreneurs think that it is easy to measure the effectiveness of a C&C program. They think that effectiveness means rapid cash flow and no bad debts—simplicity itself!

Unfortunately, in this case the K.I.S.S. (Keep It Simple, Stupid) management method prohibits potential profits. If a company is to succeed, it must go beyond sure things. Not-so-fast pays and writing off bad debts is a part of doing business—that is, part of doing business profitably.

Evaluate your C&C system as a whole. Focus on your overall business profitability, rather than on specific account histories.Of course, you need to keep track of individual accounts, but keep them in their place. If you let your frustration with one or two bad apples spoil your entire C&C harvest, you will not reap your program's overall benefits. To help do this, there are many measures of C&C effectiveness, including:

- Bad debt as a percentage of sales
- Bad debt as a percentage of Accounts Receivable
- Losses in absolute dollars
- Number of bad accounts
- Number of account writedowns—how many accounts did you have to negotiate down to get any payment at all?
- Account writedowns in absolute dollars
- Account writedowns as a percentage of Accounts Receivable
- Average age of Accounts Receivable

The above measurements can be combined for more detailed analyses. For example:

- Do you have a very high *average age of Accounts Receivable,* because you are trying to reduce your number of account writedowns? Is this compromise profitable?
- Do you currently have a large *account writedown in absolute dollars*? That is not a particularly worrysome statistic *if* the losses were incurred by a small *number of bad accounts.* That being the case, you would not have a problematic trend, you would have a problem that would end. Stop doing business with the *bad accounts* and the dollar dilemma will dissolve.

Use these individual figures and combined measurements to compare your record to industry averages, competitors' figures, other local companies, etc. In those areas where you do not measure up, figure out where you went wrong.

After you have collected the C&C numbers, you will need to ask yourself some objective questions. Analyze the revenue and/or profit you are making, or not making, as a direct result of your Credit and Collection policies. This means determining:

- The percentage of your sales that are credit sales
- The percentage of your sales you are likely to lose if you eliminate credit
- The percentage of your sales you are likely to lose if you tighten credit
- The percentage of your sales you would lose if you accept only Grade A credit risks
- The percentage of your sales you would lose if you accept only Grade A and B credit risks
- The percentage of your profits that come from credit sales. Keep in mind that, by increasing overall sales, C&C helps you achieve economies of scale and reduce product costs. Therefore, cutting customer credit will endanger profits, both by reducing sales and by increasing per-unit expenses and overhead.

- The percentage of your profits you would lose if you eliminate or tighten credit
- The percentage of your profits you would lose if you accept only Grade A credit risks; if you accept only Grade A and B credit risks

Perhaps the most important factor will be to determine:

- Measurement goals you will set to maximize credit profitability

There are no easy methods to analyze your revenues and/or profits. Ignoring them will certainly not make them go away. C&C policies must be accurately and exhaustively measured to determine their effect on profitability. You must insure that your C&C program does less harm than good.

2. Non-C&C corporate conditions

C&C strategies run the gamut from conservative—a tight credit policy—to liberal—loose purse strings—to somewhere in between. Unfortunately, decisions on credit restrictions are often based—you might even say biased—on gut instinct. They should be based on *objective business conditions.*

In general, your company should offer liberal credit terms if:

- You want to open many new accounts

  Rationale: there are only so many low risk customers. If you want a bigger business, you have to take bigger risks.

- You are in a competitive industry

  Rationale: a loose credit policy may help take customers away from competitors.

- You are bringing out new products

  Rationale: customers who are unsure of a product's sale-ability (e.g., inventory turn and the resulting income) will need better credit terms.

- You have a high overhead

  Rationale: lower your per-sale overhead costs by increasing the number of sales. Increase the number of sales by loosening credit.

- You have a trendy product or service

  Rationale: move the product while it is hot by offering good credit terms.

- Your product is past its prime

  Rationale: move the product before it is too cold by offering good credit terms.

- You must have high sales volume

  Rationale: credit facilititates sales; loosening credit leads to higher sales volume.

- You have high advertising costs

  Rationale: advertising does not help if customers cannot buy your product.

- You have high sales costs

  Rationale: the sales expense is for naught if customers cannot buy your product.

- Traditionally you have high inventory levels

  Rationale: it is better to sell products on credit than have them sitting in your warehouse.

- You have a high profit margin

  Rationale: your profit margin can absorb a relatively high level of loss.

In general, your company should offer conservative credit terms if it meets these conditions:

- The demand for your product or service is greater than the supply

  Rationale: if you can pick and choose your customers, choose to go with the less risky ones.

- You sell custom products

  Rationale: you may not be able to resell a custom order. You must be sure the client will be around to pay for the product.

- Your product has a long production cycle

  Rationale: couple long production time with extended credit terms and you have excessive carrying charges.

- Your business is threatened by rough economic conditions such as recession, depression and local layoffs

  Rationale: customers are greater credit risks when there is more risk and uncertainty in the business environment.

- Your business is overextended

  Rationale: an overextended business cannot afford to extend much credit. Offering credit can be very expensive.

- Traditionally, your inventory levels are low

  Rationale: reserve the product for low credit risks, where carrying charges, oversupply, etc., are not problems.

Your internal influences are a part of your C&C environment—nothing more, nothing less. They need to be addressed with the same objective, not selective, process used on other business obstacles.

MAKING IT WORK

Having a Credit and Collections program that is based on realism—rather than idealism—requires a thorough understanding of the three R's: Research, Reform, and Report.

Most companies do a good job in the research (what affects our C&C program?) and reform (what do we do about it?) departments. Where they lose is in the reporting requirement.

Even a Credit and Collection program with a firm foundation can leave your firm floundering *if it is not communicated to customers.* Clients need to know what changes are being made and why.

Communicating C&C conditions and changes to customers can generate big benefits. Customers understand that you are ready and willing to respond to market changes and client needs. They know the reasoning that goes into your C&C department—answer the hard questions and you avoid hard feelings. They know you are serious about Credit and Collections. They know you want to keep communication channels open.

You should also remember that communication facilitates manipulation. For example, if you are instigating a fast pay discount program at the request of your customers, let them know it. You will get a better—and faster!—ROI (Return On Innovation).

The following memo shows how a form letter can perform C&C miracles.

Mr. John Q. Customer
1 Way
Thrillsville, US

Dear John:

There's only one constant in business—change!

Here at Superior Stuff, Inc., we try to make sure that when we change, it's in accordance with the wants and needs of our customers.

In response to customer demand, we've created a fast pay discount plan. As you can see by the attached Information Sheet, our fast pay discount is designed to facilitate cost effective financing.

When local banks charge 12% on business lines of credit, we adjust our fast pay discount so that you can save 13% in effective annual interest. In short, with our program, bank financing saves you money rather than costs you money!

If you have any questions or comments regarding our fast pay discount program, feel free to give me a call. In the meantime, I hope this "chump change" helps you save big bucks!

Sincerely,

James Jefferson
President

attachment

SUMMARY

If you want to build a solid foundation for your C&C program, your first concrete steps must be in research. You need to know your business environment if you are going to engineer a constructive Credit and Collections blueprint.

Knowing your business environment will allow you to:

- Build a program with an eye toward economic realities.
- Design a framework that incorporates what you know about your industry's and competitors' successful and unsuccessful programs.
- Construct a program that includes windows to let your customers' needs and wants shine in.
- Engineer your program so that it blends into your corporate landscape. Do not plan a program you cannot live with.

Thanks to environmentally sound planks, your C&C program will be a solid structure, not a house of cards.

Both positive and negative conditions are likely to impact more than the C&C function. Sales, marketing, financial planning, staff morale, etc., may all be affected. Paying attention to your C&C will pay off in more ways than one.

ASK YOURSELF

- What resources are available for researching your competitors' C&C scenarios? Which will give you the most valid information for the least amount of effort?
- What four customer issues need to be addressed before design a C&C program? Do you currently address them in your program?
- What internal business issues will influence the typical C&C system? How important are they in your business?
- What economic conditions, at both local and national levels, will have the greatest negative impact on your business?
  - How will you track them?
  - How often will you track them?
  - Who will track them?
  - What analytical process will you undertake if significant changes occur?

  Answer the same questions for positive local and national economic conditions.
- What industrial and/or competitive conditions do you anticipate will have the greatest negative impact on your business?
  - How will you track them?
  - How often will you track them?
  - Who will track them?
  - What analytical process will you undertake if significant changes occur?

  Answer these same questions for positive industrial and/or competitive conditions.

- Which customer wants, needs, compromises, etc., do you expect to have the greatest negative impact on your business?
    - How will you track them?
    - How often will you track them?
    - Who will track them?
    - What analytical process will you undertake if significant changes occur?

  Answer these same questions for the positive customer influences.
- What internal business conditions will have the greatest negative impact on your business? Identify the most potent positive conditions. You should monitor all these conditions continuously.

CHAPTER THREE

DETERMINING YOUR CREDIT TERMS

PAYMENT TERMS

Deciding what you want to offer your customers in terms of credit is the next step in developing a profitable credit program. You must be careful where you step. While the right credit terms can generate terms of endearment, the wrong ones can create long term, perhaps even terminal, problems.

As a beginning businessperson, it makes sense to keep your credit program as plain as possible. Simplicity succeeds for a variety of reasons. Basic programs are easy and expensive to administer, easy to modify and easy to sell. So when it comes to program design, easy does it best.

So ease into your credit program by making the easiest of all credit decisions: determine what credit terms you are going to offer your customers. This process has only two prongs. You need to decide what you are going to provide in the way of payment terms (e.g., net due dates, fast pay discounts, late pay finance or interest charges) and credit limits.

Your Turn

Check the research you did on your industry and competitors.

- What were the most common payment terms?
- Are they good enough for you?
- Can and should you offer more?

Payment terms are a three legged stool, with each leg as important as the other. Collectively, they put you on the hot seat. That is because well crafted payment terms can generate business and profits, while inappropriate terms potentially generate nothing but trouble.

A credit program that includes fast pay discounts, a net due date and interest charges does three important things:

1. It creates a significant financial incentive for fast payments: a fast pay discount.
2. It sets a formal deadline for payments: the net due date.
3. It provides a significant financial disincentive for slow payments: interest and finance charges.

By emphasizing one element over the others, you can manipulate or reinforce customer payment behavior. For example, if your customers could, but do not, pay immediately, you may want to stress a fast pay discount. This will encourage them to pay today, rather than pay someday. This is why you want to find your maximum mix between fast pay discounts, net pay dates and slow pay interest charges.

CAVEAT: Before you start inventing new payment terms, take a caustic look at your competitors' common payment terms. Standard industry practice exists for a good reason: it usually works fairly well. It is what customers expect. It meets the peculiar permutations of your industry. So do not reinvent the wheel unless you have a good reason. Your program may fall flat.

To find your best business balance, try to keep things simple (e.g, do not invent something new when a small innovation will do). Keep the following in mind:

FAST PAY DISCOUNTS

Before making any discount decisions, consider:

- Discounts you have offered in the past
- The effectiveness of your past and present discount program(s)
- What you think discounts should or could do for, or to, your business
- How discounts would likely effect customer behavior
- How discounts will effect your profit margin
- Discount programs offered by your competitors or in your industry
- How much of a financial *break* you can afford to give your customers
- The effect of fast pay discounts coupled with credit card charges (e.g, can you afford to offer a 2 percent fast pay discount and pay the credit card company its 4 percent?)
- The use of C.O.D. or pre-pay discounts, which should be somewhat larger than standard fast pay discounts since they virtually eliminate your credit risk

Communicate the business benefits of your discount program.

If your discount program saves clients an effective 18 or 36 percent per year, and their bank financing costs only 12 or 14 percent, it makes dollars and sense for them to use bank, rather than vendor, financing.

Spell out the potential savings (e.g., "Save money! Take advantage of our fast pay discount, which will save you 36 percent per annum on financing—less than the cost of bank financing.") Make sure your customers understand the financial implications, lest they be disinclined to accept your offer.

Of course, you must make sure that your discount program offers a real, as opposed to surreal, benefit. If bank or other financing costs less than vendor financing (see below) your buyers will pay you, rather than delay you.

Paying on the net due date and losing the fast pay discount will cost your clients (on a per annum basis):

If your terms are	Cost to clients
1/10 net 30	18%
2/10 net 30	36%
2/10 net 60	14%
2/30 net 60	24%
2/40 net 60	36%
3/10 net 30	54%
3/30 net 60	36%

NEVER allow buyers to take undeserved discounts.

Check the postmark on every remittance envelope. If a check was mailed too close to its discount deadline, rebill the customer for the discount difference.

Make it clear to your clients that they only have two choices: *earn* your discount or *spurn* your discounts. They cannot have it both ways.

NET DUE DATES

Net due dates tend to be fairly standard within any given industry. They reflect the general cash flow patterns of those within it.

You should recognize, however, that net due dates can be used to leverage decisions you make vis-a-vis fast pay discounts and slow pay interest charges. For example:

- A more prompt payment push is available with *2/10 net 30* than with *2/10 net 60*. With the first option, the customer can save 36 percent per annum; with the second, only 14 percent. If you want fast cash, but can only afford to offer a 2 percent discount, you can leverage it with a shorter net due date.

  NOTE: Even without the 2 percent discount, *net 30* is also more effective in generating cash flow than *net 60.*

- Interest charges that start to accrue at *net 30* have a more immediate impact than interest charges starting at *net 90.* Based on *net 30,* the customer starts paying interest after only a one month delay.

  NOTE: There is an additional psychological push for payment when purchasers start paying interest on their past due interest.

So when you set a net due date, make sure that it complements, rather than circumvents, the decisions you make relative to your other payment terms.

INTEREST CHARGES

Interest rates will be affected by:

- What you have charged in the past
- The effect your past program has had on your business (e.g., did charging interest cause you to lose customers? Did you have to write off interest charges? Were they more trouble than they were worth?)

- What you think interest charges could do to your sales and marketing efforts (i.e., would they limit your customer base?)
- The interest charges levied by your competitors or others in your industry

To insure that interest charges net more gain than pain:

- Charge justifiable interest rates. He who generates too much interest on his past due accounts will not generate much interest in his products.

  You can base interest rates on:

  - What you pay for bank financing
  - What your clients pay for bank financing
  - What it costs to carry your Accounts Receivable
  - The prime rate or some other common index

  Or you can choose interest rates that facilitate negotiations. For example:

  - Charge interest rates that are double what you pay for financing, then tell long overdue clients that you will cut their interest charges in half if they will pay within ten days.
  - Charge clients a higher interest rate on each successive month (e.g., 1 percent per annum the first month, 2 percent per annum the second, etc.)

Mandate a minimum interest charge (e.g., $10). Overdue charges must cover your administrative overhead.

Do not start charging interest the day a bill is past due. Give the customers a short grace period. If you do not receive a check after the grace period, charge interest dating back to the payment's due date.

The name of the game in payment terms is prompting a prompt payment. You can do that by offering the right combination of fast pay discounts, net due dates and interest charges. Together, they form the three-legged stool that tables a lot of payment problems.

CREDIT LIMITS

Credit limits are easier to set than payment terms. They can also set you up for a bigger fall. Why? Because:

- Credit limits are *customerized.*

  Customers should be offered varying credit limits in accordance with their creditworthiness. Unfortunately, when you treat customers differently you can generate differences of opinion (e.g., "Why are you offering a lower—or higher—credit limit to *X* than you are giving to the *Y* guy?")

- Credit limits are competitive.

  If you offer a potential customer less credit than he can get elsewhere, he may keep, or start, buying from Elsewhere, Inc. If you offer him much more, he may decide that you are desperate for business and be less prompt with his payments.

- Credit limits reflect the vendor's honest opinion of the buyer.

  Credit limits are, to a degree, a matter of personal ego and faith—things that matter to most customers. If you do not trust the customer with a large credit account, he may not entrust you with his purchase orders.

Approach Credit Limits With Caution

Fortunately, if you set yourself down and approach the subject cautiously, you will not set yourself up for a major credit limit fall.

Once again, first review the practices of your competitors and industry, this time with an eye toward standard credit limits. Hopefully, you will see a range of credit limits (e.g., "Customer credit limits in our industry range from $15,000 to $25,000.") that will help you start to formulate a financial focus.

Second, determine if this credit limit range makes sense for you, given your economic and business realities. Can you afford to offer $25,000 credit limits? Can you sweeten the purchasing pie by offering $30,000 or $35,000? (Why is it that your competitors only offer maximum credit of $25,000? What do they know that you do not know?)

> **NOTE:** With payment terms that include a profitable fast pay discount, short net due date and impressive interest charges, you can offer more credit because customers will take less time to pay.
>
> You can also offer higher credit limits if you have a secure competitive position (e.g., you are the only business that sells *X* in your area), a secure credit position (e.g., you insist on collateralized credit or personal guarantees), or a secure credit tracking program (e.g., you move quickly to cut off credit should a customer fumble the billing ball).
>
> Third, decide the criteria a customer will have to meet before receiving an *X* credit limit. This subject is addressed in detail in Chapters 4 and 5.
>
> **NOTE:** This step is undercut by a critical complicating factor. You must be prepared to offer credit to any businesses which meet your objective criteria. To do otherwise invites costly lawsuits (e.g., "Why are you discriminating against the plaintiff?"). It is okay to offer customers something they cannot refuse; it is not okay to offer customers something you cannot supply.

Finally, to keep your credit limit problems within limits, consider these caveats:

- Customer credit limits are not rubber bands. Do not stretch them just because a client needs to make a really big buy, simply because he asked you to, or because he threatened to take his business elsewhere. Credit limits are not granted *just because.* They are given *just for cause.*

  If you believe that a customer could handle a larger credit commitment, or that his current credit should be cut back, make the necessary changes. Otherwise, resist the temptation to trifle.

- Customers are not limited to your credit limit. If you offer a customer a $25,000 credit limit, realize that this is just the beginning. He is also getting credit from other companies.

Added together, credit *limits* can generate almost unlimited lucre. To paraphrase an old political paradigm, $25,000 here, $25,000 there, and pretty soon you are talking about real money.

Be careful not to hitch a ride on a losing bandwagon. Determine each credit customer's cumulative credit line. If you do not think he can handle the grand total, do not offer him the 25 grand. It would be a grandeous error.

- Try to tie each customer's credit limits into his average monthly purchases. If your payment terms are *net 30* and a customer spends an average of $10,000 a month, offer him a $10,000 limit. That way he is forced to stay current and you stay ahead of major collection problems.

- Credit security (such as collateralized credit, standby lines of credit, sufficiently solvent co-signers, credit insurance, personal guarantees) also tends to extend your credit program's outer limits. The more financial backing you and/or your customers have, the more you can front financially.

  Make sure, however, that all forms of security are formally reviewed and approved by your lawyer. Accept no handshake deals. To quote Sam Goldwyn, "Verbal promises aren't worth the paper they're printed on." Also make sure that the securities pledged against your accounts are not being held accountable by other security-conscious suppliers.

Credit limits may look simplistic, but if they are handled carelessly they can cause unlimited trouble. Do not offer more than you can afford and do not offer more than your customers can afford. It is as simple, and as complicated, as that.

MAKING IT WORK

If you want your credit terms to do you credit, communication again, is the key.

Many well designed credit term programs fail to live up to their profit potential; in fact, they die on the vine. Why? Because customers are not told (a) what their suppliers credit terms are and (b) how to benefit from them.

In other words, suppliers spend a great deal of time and money planning their credit term parties—then forget to send their customers any invitations! As a result, there's no R.S.V.P.—Return of Substantial Valuable Profits.

Get graphic! Forms like the following will both note and promote your credit terms.

PROMOTING DISCOUNTS

When you send out an initial invoice or billing statement, include a second pseudo "bill." This second sheet should tell the customer what he needs to pay and when, to take advantage of fast pay discounts.

For additional emphasis, print your discount deal on bright colored paper.

Customer: Superior Stuff Inc.

Invoice: 12345

If you pay the $15,550 due on the referenced invoice no later than 1/2/93*, pay only $15,394.50, a savings of $155.50!

This represents an annualized saving rate of 18%.

According to our most recent survey, local banks are charging an average of 12% on lines of credit.

Borrow from the bank, pay us early, and save 6%!

** If you plan to mail your payment, it must be postmarked a minimum of three days before the referenced date if the discount is to be allowed.*

PROMOTING INTEREST

When a payment procrastinator gets a form like this one in the mail, it gets his interest. It also encourages him to take his "loan-liness" to a bank, where it belongs.

Memo to: Superior Stuff Inc.

Memo from: Jack Johnson, President, Magnificent Materials

According to our most recent survey, local banks are charging the following interest rates on business lines of credit:

First National	12%
Second National	12.25%
Third National	12%
Fourth National	11.87
Fifth National	12%
Sixth National	12%

And what do we charge on past due accounts? 18%!!!!!

Clearly, our financing doesn't do you any favors. That's why I suggest you favor a local bank with your borrowing business. Their more favorable financing rates mean a higher rate of return for your business.

SUMMARY

What you offer customers in the way of payment terms and credit limits will affect what they offer you in terms of business. For long term success, you must insure that your offering is competitive, concise, current and cost-effective. In other words, your C&C program must be C&C&C&C to succeed.

ASK YOURSELF

- What are the two components of any credit offering? Which is of more importance to your business?

  NOTE: While some industries stress payment terms over due dates, and visa versa, a strong case can be made for either perspective.

  What are the three goals of a successful credit program? Does your own program meet these goals?

  What are the main issues relevant to offering fast pay discounts? Do you address them in your program?

- How can a business leverage net due dates to reinforce their credit parameters? How does your net due date impact what you are trying to accomplish via fast pay discounts or slow pay interest charges?

- What are the main issues relevant to charging interest on past due accounts? Do you charge interest because "everybody else does," or do you use interest charges to further your business and C&C plan?

- What are the major points to consider before setting specific credit limits? Are they addressed in your specific program?

- What do your top ten competitors do, relative to fast pay discounts? If possible, determine:

  - Each competitor's rationale behind his fast pay discount decision
  - Whether his apparent rationale holds water
  - If not, whether you can leverage his mistake(s) into your own C&C opportunity

- What do your top ten competitors do, relative to net due dates?

  - Do their programs make sense?
  - If not, is there anything you can do, relative to net due dates, which will strengthen your competitive position?

- What do your top ten competitors do, relative to interest charges on past due bills? Consider:
  - Charging lower interest rates. If you can afford to float critical customers for a month or two, charging less interest will attract the "I can pay, but not today" crowd.
  - Charging higher interest rates. Higher interest charges will not be a major issue if the vast majority of your customers pay within your established net due dates. It will, however, be a strong motivational tool for those who let their payments slide. In short, you can probably motivate the slow payers without aggravating the fast payers.
- What do your top ten competitors do, relative to customer credit limits? Determine the rationale behind their credit limits:
  - If the limits appear unreasonably high, are your competitors doing something that you are not (e.g., requiring personal financial guarantees, standby lines of credit, second signatures? Do they know something that you do not (e.g., perhaps they have a better information base from which to make their C&C decisions)?

    If the limits appear unreasonably low, do they offer you a potential competitive advantage, and do you have the financial wherewithal to access it? A competitor may offer lower credit limits because he has information on upcoming industry problems. He may offer less than you do, because he knows more than you do. It is something to consider.

CHAPTER
FOUR

DEVELOPING YOUR CREDIT APPLICATION FORM

CREDIT APPLICATION FORMS PROVIDE FOR YOU

Many beginning businesspeople treat their credit application form merely as a credit formality, as an administrative annoyance. That is unfortunate, because he who fails to collect the right credit information, from the right people, at the right time, in the right way, finds himself practicing credit and *collections*, rather than *credit* and collections. He finds himself dealing with problems instead of making deals with customers.

Application forms are important because:

- They provide your first objective insight into a customer's character, creditworthiness, capabilities, etc. They allow you to test your initial personal and professional impressions against objective information.
- They provide your best insight into a firm's financial foundation. Customers are more responsive, more willing to provide sensitive dollars-and-cents information during the initial credit application process than they will be at any other time. This opportunity knocks but once, and the wise entrepreneur knocks himself out to take advantage of it.
- They often provide all the information you need to spot bogus businesses and other flagrant frauds. (This subject will be covered in depth in Chapter 5.)
- They provide both credit tools (i.e., the information you need to measure a customer's creditworthiness) and collection tools (i.e., the information you need to collect on past due accounts).

In short, credit application forms *provide* for you. Period.

CREDIT APPLICATION INFORMATION

This information gathered via credit application forms falls into three main categories:

1. General (i.e., the "name, rank and serial number" variety)
2. Financial
3. Reference

Most credit application forms, even the bad ones, address these three main areas. The trick is to request the right information, relevant to all of these categories.

Start the credit application design process by reviewing your research. Gather any credit application forms you have on hand. Augment your collection with selections from:

- Your vendors
- Your customers
- Your competitors—you can usually get these from your customers
- Non-geographic *competitors*—people in your industry, but not in your geographic market
- Credit organizations (e.g., the National Association of Credit Managers)
- Local credit cooperatives
- Credit reporting agencies
- Relevant business or professional organizations (e.g., National Federation of Independent Businesses, American Society of Software Consultants)
- The generic forms section of your local stationery store

Once you amass a mess of samples, find the form that looks most appropriate for your business. Chances are, it will be one from a competitor or industry specialist. Your task will be to improve it; it will provide a skeletal structure that you can flesh out into your own customized credit application form.

There is no one *best* credit form. There is, however, the credit form that is best for your business. You will create it yourself by besting the most appropriate form you find. Reform your form one careful step at a time.

GENERAL INFORMATION

This section does not change much from industry to industry, but it probably needs much in the way of change. Most forms collect the basically trite and bypass the enlightening information facts that can help you avoid payment problems and con artists. The importance of this information and how to use it, will be covered in Chapter 5.

Yes, you need to collect basic information (i.e., name, address, phone, etc.), but that is not enough. Your credit application form should also address:

Credit Terms

You must inform your customers up front—that is, as part of the credit granting process—that they are obligated to pay their bills in accordance with your sales terms (relative to payment terms, freight or insurance charges, etc.), and that they will be required to pay any collection and/or court costs associated with their account.

This must be done via the initial application form. Statements made *after the fact* (e.g., after the purchase) on billing statements or in collection letters have no legal authority. The customer's signature on your credit application form is their legal sign of acceptance and approval.

Executive Officers of a Business

As a minimum, you need to know:

- The names of major executives
- Where and how they can be contacted during office hours
- Where and how they can be contacted after office hours

In many small organizations, the owner and company may be all but indistinguishable. In a single proprietorship, they are legally one and the same. In this case, you will be making a credit decision based not on the company itself, but on the company *and* the owner—his or her character, his or her business and professional abilities, his or her background, his or her assets. You will need to know the following about the owner (and his or her spouse if they reside in a community property state):

- Social security number(s)
- Driver's license number(s)

- Credit card number(s)
- Professional and trade license or registration numbers
- Professional affiliations
- Alma mater(s)
- Personal assets, liabilities, informal and formal obligations
- Personal and professional references
- Intricacies of ownership

It is not enough to know if a potential customer is a sole proprietorship, partnership or corporation. You need enough additional information to judge the customer's credit credibility. Following are a few examples:

- This credit applicant is a partnership. In addition to the usual questions (e.g., who are the partners? are they working partners? how long have they been partners?), you need to find out:
    - What happens to the business if one of the partners is killed or incapacitated?
    - How, specifically, will changes in the legal structure of the business be financed (e.g., via treasury certificates, stock, life insurance proceeds)? Have the financial instruments been pledged elsewhere as collateral? Who controls them and where are they?
- This credit applicant is a wholly owned subsidiary of a parent company with a lot of money. Does that provide security for you? That depends. Will the parent company co-sign its subsidiary's account? What is the parent company's personal profit position? To insure the value of a parent companys's co-signature:
    - Insist that all guarantees are legitimate. The parent company should provide a standing resolution or certificate of resolution to document that the person or committee who provided the co-signature was duly authorized.

      The standing resolution or certificate of resolution should not be signed by the same person who signed the guarantee. This suggests personal, rather than corporate, empowerment.

- Verify the parent company's credit record. A co-signature is worthless if the co-signator has less worth than expected.

Processing Information

To avoid purchasing, billing and delivery problems, ask your customer:

- Who has the authority to make a purchase?
- Who is responsible for the Accounts Payable Department?
- Who has the authority to process a payment and cut a check?
- Who should be called if there is a payment problem?
- Who should receive the bill (e.g., "ATTN: John Doe, Accounts Payable")?
- What is the billing address? Is it the same as the delivery address?
- How many copies of the bill do you need? Should all copies be sent to the same address?

The personal information you require will vary, depending on how important the business principals are to your credit granting decision. If, for example, the business is incorporated, little personal information is necessary.

Your Turn

Analyze your credit application form to determine:

- General information you currently collect.
- Additional general information that would be of value in your credit granting decisions. Most likely, this will be personal information, relative to the applicant's business principals.
- Is this additional information pertinent to your C&C decision? Never make an informational request that you cannot defend; requiring personal information is already a touchy subject with some subjects.

FINANCIAL INFORMATION

A financial disclosure requirement forces your credit applicant to put his money where his mouth is. Sure, he can tell you how well his business is going and growing, how secure he and his finances are. He can assure you that his business is well run and not being run into the ground. He can claim he makes money faster than he can spend it.

He can tell you whatever fact or fiction he likes. After all, words come cheap. His financial disclosure, however, will tell it like it is. As they say, money talks. You had better listen to what it has to say.

When collecting financial information, insure that:

1. You collect the right information
2. The information you collect is right

These two items are not the same.

To insure that you collect the right information:

- Provide your applicant with a framework form for each financial report you require. Depending on you and your industry, these could include a balance sheet, Profit & Loss Statement, operating statement, etc. Break down the columns into whatever categories are most meaningful to you and/or to others in your industry.

  For example, imagine that businesses in your industry have a difficult time collecting their Accounts Receivables. This is due mostly to their customers' own overextended Accounts Receivables. Therefore, a critical financial element to collect vis-a-vis your applicants is the breakdown, by age, of their Accounts Receivables.

  On most credit applications, customers are asked to state their Accounts Receivables as an aggregate figure (e.g., $100,000). Due to your industry's special circumstances, your form should require a further Accounts Receivables breakdown. For example:

Accounts Receivables	$ Amount
less than 30 days old	$5,000
30-59 days	$10,000
60-89 days	$15,000
90-119 days	$40,000
120 days old	$30,000
Total Accounts Receivables	$100,000

- Define your terms. You will not get the right information if your applicants misunderstand what you want.

  Using the prior example, in place of asking for "Accounts Receivables figures," define what you mean by Accounts Receivables. Does aggregate Accounts Receivables include the interest charges on past due accounts? Does it include contested bills? Is this Accounts Receivables figure offset elsewhere by product returns? Does Accounts Receivables include fees that will not be collected in cash (e.g., services provided in a barter arrangement)?

To insure that the information you collect is accurate:

- Insist on at least two audited financial statements. These should be forwarded to you by the company's outside accountant, to ensure that numbers have not been improved or removed. Always read a financial report's pursuant memorandum or footnotes. That is usually where accountants tactfully hoist their red flags.

  NOTE: Make sure that the two audited reports are of the same type. You will want to compare two balance sheets, for example, so that you can spot trends and/or trickery.

- Insist on at least twelve consecutive financial statements. This increases the odds of accuracy, particularly if you are comparing the company's internal reports with external, audited reports of the same timeframe. It is much more difficult to fake a run of financial statements than it is to run off a single fraudulent form.

Your Turn

Check the financial section of your credit application form:

- What information do you currently require?
- What additional information might help you make a more informed C&C decision? Do you simply want more data, or are you looking for substantiation, verification, etc.?
- What can you do to insure that the financial information you receive is the right information?
- What can you do to insure that the financial information you receive is accurate?

CREDIT REFERENCES

The one major flaw in collecting credit references is that no applicant would ever willingly give you a bad one.

Fortunately, there is one major hurrah in collecting credit references—you can, with a little luck and a lot of strategy, force applicants to tip their hands in a way that will tip you off to potential trouble.

You do that by requiring applicants to provide particular types of references. For example:

- *Require credit applicants to list their three major vendors.* These references will probably be specialty vendors with a strong track record in the applicant's industry. Their judgment of the applicant (his creditworthiness, business abilities, future in the industry, etc.) should be very sound.
- *Require credit applicants to list several small generic suppliers.* A good measure of a company's credit character is to see how it treats those small suppliers (printers, stationery stores, janitorial services, florists, etc.) who could easily be replaced.
- *Require credit applicants to supply the name of at least one vendor who has refused to give them credit.* You will want to

determine why the applicant was denied credit. Does this other vendor know something you do not?

- *Require credit applicants to give you the name of the vendor you are replacing.* Did the applicant switch suppliers because he preferred your product, or because he deferred too many of your predecessor's bills?

Your Turn

Answer the following:

- What are the four primary reasons that credit application forms are important? Does your business use credit applications for these purposes?
- What are the three major categories of credit application information? Do all three appear on your application form?
- What criteria should be set in gathering worthwhile general information?
- What vendor terms must be communicated on the initial credit application?
- What specific information must be gathered if the applicant is a wholly owned subsidiary?
- What processing information do you request on your application form?

Review your credit application form to determine if you are asking for:

- Enough credit references
- The appropriate credit references
- The right reference information

As you analyze your competitors' credit application forms, ask yourself:

- What information do they request?
- How much information do they request?

What, and how much, information they gather will tell you what they value and what they will use in making credit granting decisions.

- What can you learn from this?

MAKING IT WORK

Want to see some magic? You can turn your credit application form into—abracadabra!—a collection curmudgeon!

It is easy. You do not need any slight of hand, just a slightly unusual strategy.

Express—and stress—the importance of collections by treating your credit application seriously, like it is a critical business contract—which it is. You should:

- Alway print your credit application form on expensive watermark paper. Use impressive, but somewhat unusual type. This emphasizes its importance and reduces the possibility of fraud (e.g., customers would have a difficult time replacing your original sheets with altered others).

  NOTE: Never send out dog-eared application forms. That is not how one "puts on the dog!"

- Highlight, with a colorful marker, the most important information (For example: you are required to pay all invoices in full within 30 days of the billing date indicated on the invoice. . . .").
- Have the applicant initial all highlighted areas, and have his initials either notarized or witnessed.
- Have the applicant and the company sales rep (or collection staffer) discuss and initial all contract pages.
- Provide the applicant with a self addressed, stamped envelope for his completed application.

  NOTE: Because mailing fraudulent financial facts is a felony, inform the client that all financial information must be sent via the U.S. Post Office. Thus, you up the ante on any scurrilous scam).

- Always send countersigned/accepted application forms by Registered Mail.
- Stamp each page with the words "LEGAL CONTRACT."
  - You can even replace the words "CREDIT APPLICATION FORM" with "CREDIT CONTRACT" or "BINDING CREDIT AGREEMENT."

SUMMARY

When you design your credit application, there is enough room for a slew of signatures. You will want your form to be signed by the major corporate officers. Likely candidates include: Chief Executive Officer, President, Chief Financial Officer, Vice President of Legal Affairs. You will also want to get signatures of two witnesses.

At a minimum, witness signature blocks should contain:

- Name
- Corporate title and/or other affiliation
- Business address
- Business phone
- Home address
- Home phone
- Social security number
- Driver's license number
- Professional and trade license number

Why do you need this much information on witnesses? First, you want them to know that countersigning a legal document is a serious matter. Second, if it should become necessary, you want to be able to locate witnesses in the future.

ASK YOURSELF

- How does your business ensure that it gets the right financial information from applicants?
- How does your business ensure that it gets accurate financial information from applicants? Specifically, how do you ensure that the information is legitimate, from a legitimate company?

CHAPTER
FIVE

EVALUATING CREDIT APPLICATIONS

USING THE INFORMATION

Do you neglect what you collect?

Many businesspeople collect substantial amounts of information via their credit application forms, only to have the information collect dust. Their research efforts suggest *due diligence,* but because they do not know what to do with the data they gather, they do nothing with it.

The problem? Analysis paralysis. What does it all mean? Which information is important and which is impotent? How does an entrepreneur separate the credit applicants who are great from those who are second rate? What do you do when half of your information about an applicant suggests a thumbs up, while the other half suggests that something is wrong?

Fortunately, analyzing credit application forms is a relatively simple, relatively painless and straightforward process. You need to follow these basic keys for analysis:

Know what you are looking for.

Know where you are likely to find it.

First things first. What are you looking for? Two things, actually. You want to verify that your applicant has:

- Legitimacy—that is, you want to insure that he is not a member of some con artist Fraud Squad. If an applicant meets any of the following criteria, use extra scrutiny on his or her credit application:
    - The client, or his references, has a business name that is suspiciously (i.e., intentionally) similar to that of a well known, legitimate business.
    - The customer plans to buy items that are notoriously easy to sell on the black market (e.g., casual commodities, expensive non-custom items, items sans serial numbers, popular or hard to get products).
    - The customer should not want/need your product, (e.g., his business is unrelated to your industry, he already carries your competitor's complete line, he can buy a similar product less expensively from a closer supplier).

- The customer's business is either rush or unsolicited, you did not find the customer, he found you—at a trade show, through a catalog, after your salespeople stopped calling on his business, through an unnamed source).
- The firm has been in business less than two years (a typical fraud timeline).

► Creditworthiness—you want to verify that he has what it takes, both in terms of finances and character, to take care of his down-the-road debts.

Where will you find the information and verification you need? Some will come from the completed credit application form. You will get the rest from outside sources.

The following procedures will turn what is often a frightening analytical process into an enlightening one.

EVALUATING GENERAL INFORMATION

General information is generally used for three purposes:

1. To integrate the buyer's needs into the supplier's system

One of the best ways to avoid collection problems is to avoid billing problems. Ask your customers up front to give you the information you need for proper processing. Sending the right number of bills to the right people at the right address, for example, is the right move, both in terms of customer service and Accounts Receivables facilitation.

2. To spot frauds

Check the information you received on the credit application form against information you glean from outside sources—that is, sources outside the applicant's control. You will want to verify, compare and contrast. Most of all, question.

Of paramount importance:

► Check all of the applicant's proprietary and legal information—names of owners and executives, form of ownership, corporate address(es), Employer Identification

Number, years in business, etc.—with your State Commerce Department. The records should be totally consistent with each other.

- Verify the applicant's telephone number via the telephone company. If the phone company has never heard of the company, it is not a sound credit risk.
- Visit the applicant's place of business. This is particularly important if materials are picked up rather than delivered, if goods are shipped out of state, or if purchases are being forwarded to an address other than the billing address. If the applicant's legal address, including zip code, does not exist, desist further consideration.
- Call local credit organizations. The National Association of Credit Managers (NACM), a national affiliate of locally owned credit organizations, is a good bet; if no NACM office services your area, try local credit cooperatives. Most conscientiously maintain a list of known frauds, cross referenced by both company and executive names. Does the business name, or any of the executives' names, receive a black eye from one of these blacklists?

  Keep your own list of no-good names. You will be surprised to find that people, and even companies, who have given you financial problems in the past will keep turning up, like the proverbial bad penny.
- Check the executive's personal information, (e.g., Social Security number, driver's license number, driver's license number, professional and trade license or registration numbers) with proper authorities. If it is correct, this information will be very useful in tracking down the applicant, should he or she disappear. Of course, if the information has been falsified, you have likely identified a con artist.

3. To identify potential C&C protection

If the businessowner claims to own more than the business, or own more than the business does, consider requesting a personal financial guarantee. Why? It gives additional importance to your invoices.

The premise here is that when a business is going under, the guarantor or businessowner will sink every penny the business has into paying off your account. It is either that, or pay your bill out of his own pocket. No failed executive wants an old supplier to acquire his personal property.

A Word of Caution

Before trying to attach, or otherwise snatch, additional security from clients, consult your lawyer. As noted earlier, personal guarantees should be read and approved by a professional. Have your lawyer draw up a formal guarantee. If a lawyer would be too expensive and you want to do it yourself, perhaps with the help of some stationery store samples, *do not.*

If after reading this, if do-it-yourself is still your plan of attack, be advised that a personal guarantee should include the following, to maximize its legal leverage:

- Recognition that the guarantee is a personal, not professional one. The word *personal* should be included after the signator's—and, if relevant, his or her spouse's—typed name on the guarantee's signature line.

  Require a parallel personal guarantee from the executive's spouse if either one legally resides, owns property or does business in a community property state.

- Financial reports, personal and professional references, credit checks, outstanding guarantees, etc., relative to the signator. Give signators the same scrutiny you give the applicant's business.
- Cutoff points—examples:
  - "This personal guarantee covers all service and/or product purchases (including standard add-on charges such as delivery, travel, collection and/or finance charges and insurance) made prior to *X* date."
  - "The account must be paid in full, either by the firm or the signator, should the following business conditions occur: the signator sells the business, the signator leaves the business, there is a significant degradation of the business' financial ratios. (For example, . . .)"

Clearly, general credit application information can have specific repercussions. If you find that an applicant is not being open with you, close the book on him. His word is not binding. And if you find that the business owner has significant financial assets, do some binding of your own.

EVALUATING FINANCIAL INFORMATION

Sometimes it is difficult to get credit applicants to part with their favorite financial records. Still, sharing such secrets is the first step toward a meaningful business relationship between you and the customer.

If an applicant willingly forwards his financials, that says a lot. But it does not say enough. You still must check for potential fraud and firm finances. Again, the process is relatively straightforward.

Check for Fraud

- Check the applicant's audited financial statements. Were they compiled by a legitimate CPA (e.g., one that is listed in the telephone book and has heard of your client)?

  Verify that your applicant did not bastardize a legitimate financial report by altering—usually moving up—its date. A firm that was firm in the past may be on shaky ground today.

- Order a credit report on the applicant from a reputable credit reporting organization. Examples: National Association of Credit Managers, Dun and Bradstreet and TRW. Never rely solely on financial information from credit reporting companies. Despite the companies' best efforts, information is too often inaccurate, incomplete and inappropriate. Basically, they provide the information they have been supplied.

  Instead, use these credit reports to double check the information you receive on credit applications. When you double check, it is less likely that you will be double crossed.

Are the financial figures supplied by the applicant consistent with information provided in the credit report? If there are any differences, could they be—are they—legitimate?

Potential red flags for financial fraud include:

- The general information on your credit application does not match the general information on the credit report. For example, the address or phone number is different.
- The information on the credit report is in exactly the same order as the information on the credit application. The applicant may be working from the credit report, rather than from his own records, because the credit report is not really his.
- The credit report suggests business irregularities. For example:
  - The applicant has no record, good or bad, with the credit reporting company. While this is possible in the case of a very young company, it is hard to make a credit case for any company that fails to leave a financial track.
  - The client has an atypical history. For example, he exhausts his credit limits very quickly. Perhaps the company is atypical because it is being run like a typical fraud.
  - The report shows no old accounts, all were opened recently. The applicant is potentially a fraud.
  - Many other suppliers have requested credit reports on this applicant. The applicant may be lining up creditors so that he can quickly line his pockets with ill gotten gains.

Check for Financial Firmness

Financial analysis can get unbelievably convoluted. What is *convolute* is not necessarily *astute.*

You can test a client's financial waters without getting in too deep. Simply use *standard industrial ratio* analysis. Most credit managers apply these rules of thumb to put a finger on their applicant's basic fiscal soundness.

First, go to your local public or university library and find either the *Almanac of Business and Financial Ratios* or Dun and Bradstreet's *Industry Norms and Key Business Ratios.*

These reference texts will give you the standard financial ratios for businesses in your industry. The five most common are defined below.

Second, use your calculator to calculate your applicant's financial ratios. Compare his figures to the industry standards. If his figures are average or better, you can figure he is fiscally fit.

These five ratios are generally enough to rate an applicant:

$$\frac{\text{Total Liabilities}}{\text{Total Assets}} = \textbf{DEBT RATIO}$$

$$\frac{\text{Cash, Marketable Securities, \& Accounts Receivable}}{\text{Current Liabilities}} = \textbf{QUICK RATIO}$$

$$\frac{\text{Current Assets}}{\text{Current Liabilities}} = \textbf{CURRENT RATIO}$$

$$\frac{\text{Cost of Sales}}{\text{Inventory}} = \textbf{INVENTORY TURNOVER}$$

$$\frac{\text{Net Sales}}{\text{Average Accounts Receivable}} = \textbf{RECEIVABLES TURNOVER}$$

Financial analysis is as simple as "two bits, four bits, six bits, a dollar"—that is, if you use a little bit of common sense and a lot of outside verification.

EVALUATING CREDIT REFERENCES

Generating germane references takes genuine ingenuity. You will need to do two things:

- Ask the right questions.
- Ask the right people the right questions.

Actually, you need to ask the right people the right questions *at the right times.* That is times—plural. You need to check credit references both during the initial granting process *and on an ongoing basis.*

Once a year—or more often—if you are in a volatile industry—check in with an applicant's credit references to verify current status. Ask four simple questions:

- Do you currently solicit business from this customer?
- Has this customer's account status changed significantly since we last talked?
- Has the customer modified his payment or purchasing behavior? If the answer is *yes,* has his payment or purchasing behavior improved or gotten worse?
- Would you be willing to give this customer a higher credit limit? If so, how much higher would you go? If not, why not?

This fast-and-easy follow up should keep you from getting burned. It is a good acid test.

The more right you are, the less likely you are to be left holding a bad-account bag.

The right questions are easy to write up on a Reference Form. You need to know:

- General business information such as the customer's name, address, phone, account number, age of the account, etc. Again, you will compare what you get from the reference to what you got from the applicant. If they are not the same, the applicant may be borrowing some other business' account history.

- Financial information such as the customer's credit limit, payment terms, relevant personal guarantees and/or collateral. This information will help you determine:
  - If the applicant is being honest with you.
  - The credit limit you should offer the applicant (e.g., does the applicant have higher or lower credit limits than you would have offered? Why? Is a low credit limit a function of an overly cautious reference or the function of an overburdened applicant?)
- Payment practices and history of whether the customer pays C.O.D. or via a credit card. (e.g., does he usually take advantage of fast pay discounts? Does he typically pay within the net due dates? Does he commonly compound interest? Does he have a high level of returns, cancelled or downsized orders, etc.?) In short, will he be a cash flow problem or a cash flow solution?
- Reference history, including the last time you gave this customer a credit reference. How often do you provide a credit reference for this customer? Are the requests usually related to new accounts or expanded credit limits?

  WARNING: A heavy reference user is a likely credit abuser. Chances are, the applicant wants to cut some big purchase orders before he cuts and runs.
- The answers, if you can get them, to leading questions (e.g., is there anything about the client that you know now that you wish you had known sooner? When was the last time you increased this client's credit limit? Would you increase it now if he asked you to? Would you give this client credit without his personal guarantee? Is the applicant a personal friend of the boss?)

Asking questions is not enough. You have to discreetly question the integrity of the references who answer them.

Finding the right people to ask the right questions can be difficult. You need to:

- Question the references provided by the applicant, keeping an eye and ear open for anything that smells fishy.

- Find references not provided by the applicant, including businesses that are more likely to come clean with interesting dirt.

Questioning the applicant's references means asking general reference questions, as discussed above, and addressing fraud-specific subjects.

Penetrating the Fraud Facade

It is often easy to penetrate the fraud façade. Try these:

- Visit the reference's business. Does it even exist?

  If the address provided for a reference is a Post Office Box, make sure it is not one associated with a known mail drop. Ask your local postmaster or credit co-op. (See "Making It Work" on page 81 for more about credit co-ops.)

  CAVEAT: Never accept an address-only reference. The mail might be routed to the applicant, who would naturally offer himself a glowing reference.

- Call the reference business. Is it listed with the phone company? Is the reference telephone number that of an answering service? Did you get an answering machine, despite the fact that you called during standard business hours? Has the telephone been disconnected without a referral number? Did the person who answered the phone use a company name or just say "Hello?" Did a child pick up the receiver? Did you hear kitchen or other appliances in the background?

  CAVEAT: Never accept a phone-only reference. It, too, might be forwarded to the applicant.

- Compare the reference's names, personal and business, with fraud lists. (See "Evaluating General Information" on pages 70-73.) Does the reference company come complete with a bad frame of reference?

- Insist on reference verification. Will the reference provider send you a personalized business card with his name? Will he let you talk with another employee? Will he give you the applicant's account number so you can, secretly, verify it and the reference via another employee?

Your Turn

Answer the following:

- If you have had a credit application that was fraudulant, was the problem information or verification?
- Would the problem have been avoided or minimized had you put more effort into verifying the information you were given?

Once you have checked out the applicant's references, you need to check things out on your own. It should go without saying that if the references are no good, neither is the applicant. Leverage what you know from the applicant and what you know about the applicant, to find potentially-less-than-positive references. This requires a decidedly indirect approach. You should:

- Call the references you were given by the credit applicant. Ask them to check their records, and tell you the businesses *they* were given as credit references. Call these other businesses and see what they have to say about your applicant. Do they still do business with him or is their mutual business at a standstill? Would they still offer him credit? Continue with the standard reference questions until you get the answers, good or bad, that you need.

  While you are at it, ask these indirect references to check their records for the applicant's oldest audited financial statements. Who was the CPA of record? Is he still the applicant's CPA? If not, why not?
- Call the applicant's likely suppliers. If you know that he uses a lot of a specific product, call the companies that carry it. Did, or do, any of them supply your applicant? If so, sew up your investigation by asking the standard reference questions.
- Call the credit associations that serve your area. Some keep a complete list of their member's customers, and/or credit conflicts. Do their files indicate, or can they help you eradicate, potential problems?
- Call your commercial banker and request a bank-to-bank reference on the applicant. Bankers often share sensitive information that will have you smiling all the way to the bank.

NOTE: Provide your banker with a copy of the credit application. This legitimizes and verifies your need for the reference and provides your banker with specific customer information he needs to process your request.

Asking these businesses your standard reference questions sets the standard for savvy scrutiny. If you are lucky, they will provide additional insight into the applicant's character, or lack thereof.

Credit references, particularly when used in conjunction with general information and financial analysis, provide a good frame of reference for analyzing credit applicants. If good references have good things to say about an applicant, you have the goods on him or her. And *know* news is good news.

Your Turn

Look at the credit application forms you have received over the last six months. Separate out the credit application forms that you received from customers who subsequently did not, or could not, meet your payment terms.

- Is there anything in the general information section that could, or should, have tipped you off? If not, is there additional information you could, or should, collect that would help?
- Is there information you could have collected in the financial information section that would have helped?
- Is there anything in the credit reference section that could, or should, have tipped you off? If not, is there additional information you could, or should, collect that would help?

Study the credit applications you received from any out-and-out frauds. Hopefully, they were nothing more (e.g., also customers). But, if they were:

- Is there anything in the general information section that could or should have tipped you off? If not, is there additional information you could, or should, collect that would help?
- Is there anything in the financial information section that could, or should, have tipped you off? If not, is there

additional information you could, or should, collect that would help?

- Is there anything in the credit reference section that could or should have tipped you off? If not, is there additional information you could, or should, collect that would help?

MAKING IT WORK

When dealing with credit reports, financial reports or business references, accuracy is a big deal. That's why enterprising entrepreneurs use—you guessed it!—communication to make sure that their credit decisions are based on facts, not farce.

How do they do it? They create a local credit co-op. Specifically, a local credit co-op is a group of people representing businesses in the same—or related—industries, who meet to collect and disperse meaningful information on their common customer base. Running a credit co-op is relatively simple, if you follow these basic rules:

- The group exists only to collect, compile and exchange credit experience information—period. As a result, only people who handle these functions in a business are allowed to participate.
- Co-op members include only those firms that deal specifically with the industry in question. For example, a credit-coop consisting of members in the construction industry might include general contractors, subcontractors, lumber yards, plumbing and electrical wholesalers, floor covering and paint retailers, rental companies and bankers.
- Members are required to provide complete credit information on a regular basis and attend regular group meetings. Credit co-ops are based on the premise, "United we stand, divided we fall." All members must give and take complete information if the co-op is to fulfill its function. To do otherwise would be to give—or take—unfair advantage of the "partnership."

- Members only discuss past and completed transactions. All information is held strictly confidential and is used only for credit—never for sales or marketing—purposes. In short, members may take advantage of the co-op's valuable information, but not of their fellow members.
- There is never any agreement, express or implied, to restrict free competition or deny credit. THIS IS EXTREMELY IMPORTANT. The group never determines who can or cannot receive credit; it only informs members of who has or has not maintained a good credit record.

If this networking arrangement sounds good to you, the National Association of Credit Managers (NACM) has some sound suggestions for its management. In particular, the NACM has published a pamplet that will help your group avoid any anti-trust activities or problematic policies.

You can get a copy of the *Group Credit Policies* pamphlet by writing to the National Association of Credit Managers at 8815 Centre Park Drive, Suite 200, Columbia, MD, 21045, or by calling the organization at (301) 740-5560. You will find the phone number for your local NACM chapter in Appendix II.

A local credit group is more than a credit and collections coffee klatch. It's sort of a financial neighborhood watch. It helps you—and your peers in related industries—keep an eye out for possible procrastinators. It also helps prevent problems: purchasers who know they are being watched will see to it that their bills are paid on time.

SUMMARY

Analyzing credit application forms is relatively straightforward. You have two goals:

- Insure that your applicant is giving you the straight scoop, not offering you a crooked deal.
- Insure that your applicant is not in dire financial straits.

Leveraging common sense and outside information sources, you can meet both goals with minimum effort and maximum payoff.

ASK YOURSELF

- What are the two basic keys for successfully analyzing credit application forms? Are these incorporated into the design and use of your forms?
- What are the two things you need to look for on each credit application? Do you make a specific effort to do this in every instance?
- What are the three uses for a credit application's general information? Is your form, and your C&C program, designed to take advantage of all three?
- What five pieces of general information should always be verified through outside sources?
- What are the three critical components of a successful personal guarantee?
- What two things must you look for in the financial information?
- What are the three *red flags* of financial fraud?
- What is the *debt ratio?*
- What is the *quick ratio*?
- What is the *current ratio*?
- What is the *inventory turnover ratio*?
- What is the *receivables turnover ratio*?
- How do you use the five aforementioned ratios?
- What is the business function of a credit reporting company, and how does it affect the way you use its data?
- What are the two steps inherent in generating meaningful credit references?
- What are the five categories of information you should gather from credit references?
- Why should you refuse phone-only or address-only credit references?
- Why should you access indirect credit references?
- How do you access indirect credit references?
- What questions should you ask credit references on an ongoing basis?

CHAPTER SIX

GENERATING AND CONTROLLING YOUR ACCOUNTS RECEIVABLE

DEVELOP A SYSTEM TO MAKE IT WORK

Initially, much of what needs to be done vis-a-vis Credit and Collections is mechanistic *make work*. For a while, you are a man or woman on the make: making, if necessary, an important attitude change; making the effort to research your business environment; making critical credit term decisions; making up credit application forms; and, eventually, making sense out of them.

Well, enough *make work*. It is time to make money. Of course, that means making provisions to do so.

Do not make this process any more complicated that necessary. As an emerging entrepreneur, it is important that you develop a simple system that can control both your billing and collections processes. Your goal should be to devise a program that works almost automatically. You do not need the job of CEO—Collector of Every Overdue—or VIP—Valiant Invoice Processor. What you need is a system that does these jobs for you, one that survives via classic clerk work.

Essentially, your system needs to do two things:

- Generate billing statements
- Control accounts (e.g., keep track of who paid what, when and against which account)

Chances are, you can use a personal computer and off-the-rack software to rack up C&C success. Computer consultants and specialty publications can help you identify software specifically designed for your industry and/or desired level of C&C sophistication. See *Ulrich's Guide to Periodical Literature* for relevant computer journals. You can also contact the industry experts and organizations you found while researching your business environment.

If you are not interested in personal computer system C&C, you can still develop a system that computes. All it takes is a little system savvy.

GENERATING BILLING STATEMENTS

The billing process is not a thrilling process until you realize that this is *where money comes from.* You will find instant energy when you discover that a well designed bill can speed aggregate payments by up to 40 percent.

But first things first. Your billing process must answer to all of these basic design questions:

- Who, as in:
    - Who generates the bill? A Salesperson? Accounts Receivables clerk? Secretary?
    - Who should receive your bill? Whenever possible, bills should be addressed to a specific employee. This generates a sense of personal responsibility.
- What, as in:
    - What does the client need to know before he can approve and process your payment? Options include items ordered, unit prices, delivery date and name of purchaser.
    - What potential billing problems need to be resolved? For example, if a customer is withholding payment because of a faulty shipment, what do you do? Do you rebill as if there were no problem or hold onto your statements until the matter is resolved?
- When, as in:
    - When do bills go out? Options include: upon receipt of the order, upon shipment of the order, every Monday, and at the beginning of the month.
    - When do we stop sending bills and start sending collection letters?
- Where, as in:
    - Where does final C&C responsibility rest? Do you, the businessowner, want to take ownership for all C&C

problems? Or would you rather delegate them to a departmental delegation?

   - Where do you draw the line with customers? For example, do you accept partial payments or return them and insist that the client forward full funding?

- Why, as in:

   - Why are we doing *X*? Because other companies do it? Because it is easy? Because we have always done it this way? Or because—and this is the correct answer—it is the most efficient and cost effective approach?

   - Conversely, why aren't we doing *X*? Billing processes are like babies—they should be checked periodically, because sometimes they need to be changed.

- How, as in:

   - How do we minimize our billing risks? For example, could you verify all billing information before sending the initial invoice?

   - How do you maximize your billing efforts? For example, could you suggest that customers put their accounts on a credit card, thereby eliminating potential past due problems?

If your billing process is designed with these questions in mind, it will be a good one.

This process is only one facet of the *generate funds* function. Prompting payments is a different, but relatively simple matter of making the payment process fast and easy. For this, you need an effectively designed billing statement.

Guidelines to Speed-up Payments

According to a leading credit research organization, using the following guidelines can speed payments by up to 40 percent. To make your bill a strong statement:

- Make sure your billing statement does not look like your company's other correspondence. Do not type your bills on regular corporate letterhead.

- Emphasize important information, such as amount due or past due information, with attention-getting type. Make this type bigger, a different color, shadow blocked, darker, etc.
- Replace passive descriptions such as *Current Due* or *Due* with active commands such as *Pay Immediately* or *Pay Now.*
- Make your bill's format simple to understand. Could an eighth grade child look at the bill and answer simple questions such as: How much does the customer owe? When does he have to pay the bill? What did he buy?
- Do not put extraneous information such as company slogans, outlet addresses, advertising add-ons or brochures on or in with your billing statement. It only detracts from what is really important.
- Do not give past due columns a pre-printed position on your billing statement. This will suggest to your customers that past due accounts are a common and acceptable occurrence.
- Include any information and documentation necessary to substantiate your bill (e.g., if you charge the customer *cost plus 10%*, document the product's initial cost).
- Do not use color on your billing statement unless you have a reason (e.g., to emphasize something important).

  The specific color you use on your billing statement should be easy on the eyes (i.e., under fluorescent lights) and should come across on photocopies.

Maintain Your Image

Packaging is also important. The mailing envelope is critical. To get everything you can out of your billing envelopes:

- Send your bills in envelopes that generate attention—attention generates payment. For example, hand print the client's address or use envelopes with an engraved return address. You might also try colored stock, or have slogans printed on the outside.

Comments such as *Open Me, Do Not Fold, Act Now and Save, Dated Material, Special Offer* and *As Requested,* will elicit interest, but use them appropriately.

Comments relative to collections, such as *Overdue Bill Enclosed* or *Hey Deadbeat!* are strictly taboo.

Also, if you promise something on the outside of the envelope, such as *Savings!* or *Save unnecessary interest charges by paying this bill before . . . ,* you must deliver it inside.

► Send your clients remittance envelopes. Depending on your turnaround need, these envelopes could be:

- Self addressed
- Self addressed and stamped
- Pre-paid overnight mail (only if the payment is large or important enough to warrant the substantial cost involved).

Many businesspeople have found that faxing billing statements is an easy, inexpensive and effective alternative to the U.S. Postal Service. It is, however, a fax faux paux to transmit bills without the client's express written permission. All financial forms should be marked *Handle With Care.*

Designing an effective billing statement is the second half of the billing battle. Marshall a plan—set up a schedule for billing dates, set up a clerk to *fill the bill,* set high standards, etc.—and you have won the war.

Your Turn

Analyze your billing statement.

► How effectively does it answer all of the critical issues?

For example:

- Who?
- What?
- When?
- Where?

- Why?
- How?

If these issues are not adequately addressed, determine what charges need to be made so that it fulfills these important standards.

CONTROLLING ACCOUNTS

Beginning businesspeople need to keep a tight grip on their Accounts Receivables. One hand should be on separate client accounts, and the other should be on their aggregate amounts.

Separate Accounts

Each customer's account should be accounted for in a separate record. This record does not need to be fancy. In very basic businesses, a 3"×5" index card or a sheet of paper from an accountant's columnar pad will do.

Any specific or quantitative account actions should be listed on this card or columnar sheet. For example:

- Bills sent
- Payments made
- Fast pay discounts taken
- Interest charges levied
- Adjustments to account
- Changes in customer's account status

A simple sample account record can be found on page 101.

Keep a running total of each account; then, run a double check. The sum total of these individual accounts should be equal to the sum total on your Accounts Aging Report (see page 93).

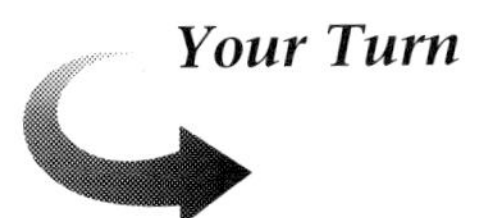

Your Turn

Randomly pick a client account card from your files. Can you see at a glance:

- Last billing date
- Last payment date
- Discount taken
- Interest charges levied
- Adjustments to account
- Changes in customer's account status

If not, determine what changes need to be made to its basic design.

Aggregate Amounts

Staying abreast of your Accounts Receivable aggregate need not aggravate. It, too, is a relatively simple process. Accounts Receivable control merely requires A Report—namely, an Accounts Aging Report.

Accounts Aging Report

An Accounts Aging (A/A) report is a summary of all amounts due. It tells you, at a glance:

- Which clients owe you money
- How much money they owe
- How much of their account balances are past due

At least once a month, at some predetermined point in time, compile a new A/A report. If you do most of your billing on the first of the month, prepare your A/A report immediately after bills are mailed.

Each month's Accounts Receivables report is, in large part, built upon the prior report. An Accounts Aging report divides each client's total amount due into time-sensitive categories. For example:

- Current
- 30-59 days past due
- 60-89 days past due
- 90-120 plus days past due

These are standard date breakdowns. If they are too broad or narrow to meet your managerial needs, revise them.

Each client's total amount due is also shown in a Total Amount Due column. Each client's current, 30-59 day, 60-89 day, 90-120+ day totals will equal his *Total Amount Due.*

Total all of the entries in the time-sensitive columns. When you add these total column figures together, you should get the same figure as when you add all of the *Total Amount Due* column figures together.

You will want to update your Accounts Aging report throughout the month, so that it provides current account insight.

- If an account is paid in full during the month, cross out that entry on the A/A report.
- If only part of the account is paid, cross off only the relevant column amount. For example, if the client paid $500 that was 60 days past due, but not the more current $1,000 due, strike the $500 from the 60 days past due column and subtract $500 from the client's line total. Note that change on the A/A report.

A sample A/A report can be found on page 102.

In larger businesses, A/A reports often serve a variety of managerial and control functions. In smaller businesses, however, A/A reports tend to do one thing—keep the business owner focused on potential collection and cash flow problems.

An A/A report includes two things: a solid report format and hints of potential trouble for the business owner. It is not difficult to spot trouble via an Accounts Aging report, if you know which spots to check. Trouble lurks in the past due columns. That is where you look for things like:

- Clients whose entire account balance, excluding interest charges, is over 60 days old

  Concerns: Have they taken their business elsewhere? Are they in such bad financial straits that they cannot make any present purchases? Has the business owner secretly skipped town or gone out of business?

- A client whose debts do not disappear until they hit the 90-120 day column

  Concerns: Why is the buyer failing to meet his contractual purchase-then-pay promises? Is the problem caused by your buyer's bureaucracy? If so, is there anything you can do to speed the paying process? Does the buyer procrastinate on payment because you do not start collection activities before the 85th day?

- Clients whose total amount due is divided among every available A/A category (e.g., some is current, some is 30-59 days, 60-89 days, etc.)

  Concerns: Why are you selling additional products to clients who have not paid past bills? Are their credit limits too high (e.g., they can purchase for months without having to make a payment)?

- A high percentage of your total Accounts Receivable is past due

  Concerns: your cash flow is barely trickling and you have to find a way to break the dam. Should you tighten your payment terms? Increase your interest charge? Institute fast pay discounts?

  NOTE: Also check for trends among the columns. For example, assume that most of the *current dues* move on to the 30-59 Days Past Due place and most then turn into 60-89 day dilemmas. However, most of the bills are paid before they hit the three month mark. Why? What are you doing to prompt payment at this point? *Could you move that special something up in the billing cycle so that it can generate even earlier payments?*

  It is not enough to spot check your A/A report for problem spots. Once you find them, you need to do some identify cleaning up. *You need to take serious action.* A/A reports can identify trouble for you, but they cannot solve it.

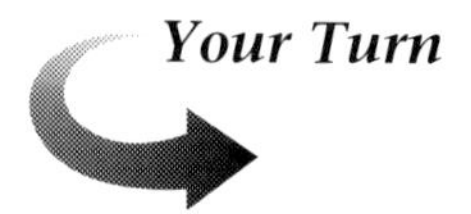

Your Turn

Take a quick glance at your Accounts Aging report. Does it help you spot problem accounts? If not, consider:

- Highlighting accounts where *X* percentage of the account or *X* dollars is over *Y* days past due
- Highlighting past due accounts where no new purchase has been made in the last few months
- Highlighting accounts where invoices are paid out of order—often a sign of financial trouble

Printing accounts with the largest past due accounts on the top—most Accounts Aging reports are organized in numerical or alphabetical order, according to account numbers or names.

MAKING IT WORK

Keeping track of Accounts Receivable means keeping *on* track. The best way to do that is to design forms that give you the right information, at the right time, in the right way.

Consider the following *Accounts Aging* form. It helps the entrepreneur (Joanne Wheeler, of Western Machine and Chrome Inc., Albany, Oregon) who designed it make sense of—and make money out of!—her Accounts Receivable. Accounts

Ms. Wheeler describes the form and its practical parts:

Form subsection: Report Type

"We compile two different kinds of *Accounts Aging* reports.

"Our first report lists all outstanding accounts. This report is available to all personnel. Our second report type is broken down by Accounts Receivable clerk. One is produced for each clerk and only lists the accounts assigned to that clerk. This report is only available to top management and the clerk in question.

"This simplifies the collection process in two ways. First, it makes sure that each clerk is aware of all his/her account responsibilities. It also gives management a comprehensive tool for following and evaluating the performance of an individual clerk."

Accounts Aging

Report Type: ______________________________

Client Type: ______________________________

Client	Total Due	Over 120	90-119	60-89	30-59	Current	Clerk Init.	P/I	Secu	Date/last Action
Interest										
Interest										
Interest										
Interest										
Interest										
Interest										
Interest										
Interest										
Interest										
Dollars Total										
Percentage										

Form subsection: Client Type

"All reports consist of at least two pages. The first page includes all accounts which may require active collection. The second page consists of municipal accounts.

"We've made this division because we don't want Accounts Receivable clerks to focus their attention and efforts on municipal clients. We know that our government clients will pay—we just don't know when.

"Assertive collection efforts won't speed up the bureaucratic payment process. They just alienate customers."

NOTE: Western facilitates municipal payments in other ways. For example, before submitting its first invoice, it asks the client how many copies of the form it needs. This saves the client unnecessary "clerk work," and helps speed payments.

Form subsection: Client

"We don't list clients by alphabetical order or according to their account numbers. We list our accounts according to outstanding balance.

"By putting the largest accounts highest on the list, the A/A form puts our collection priorities up front."

Form subsection: Interest Lines

"We generate separate interest invoices on each overdue account—which facilitates collection in court—and we list interest separately on the *Accounts Aging* form.

"There are three major benefits. First, we can see at a glance if the only activity on an account is interest-related. Second, we can make sure that no inappropriate interest is being charged (for example, to municipal customers or to customers with whom we have negotiated a partial pay agreement). Third, we know how much of a total debt—namely some percentage of the interest—we might be willing to write off in return for an immediate payment."

Form subsection: DAYS PAST DUE Columns (e.g., over 120, 90-119 days, etc.)

"Unlike most A/A forms, ours positions the *Total Amount Due* and the oldest debt categories furthest to the left. We wanted this information to be the first thing a person sees when he checks the A/A form. This way, we emphasize the dangerous debts rather than the current columns."

Form subsection: Clerk Init (Initials)

"We further identify each account by indicating which Accounts Receivables clerk is responsible for its collection.

"We initially wanted this column so that personnel could quickly identify which Accounts Receivable clerk to contact if there was a problem. Surprisingly, this column has proven to be a strong motivator. No Accounts Receivable clerk wants the recognition of having the worst or the most outstanding accounts."

Form subsection: P/I (Problem indicators)

"A simple listing of accounts doesn't tell you very much about collection complications. We wanted further insight into potential problems.

"In this column, we use an alphabetic code to communicate potential danger signs. For example:

- **P** Past problems
- **I** Invoices paid out of order (the customer didn't have enough money to pay an older, larger invoice)
- **B** Broke agreement
- **C** Changes in payment practices
- **M** Major management—or other critical personnel—changes
- **L** Total due is at or exceeds credit limit

Form subsection: Secu (Security indicators)

"A good Accounts Receivable form reports the good as well as the bad. We include this security column to identify those accounts with an additional measure of security. We try to focus first on collecting the accounts—especially the large accounts—that come to us sans security.

"Again, we use an alphabetic code to highlight the specifics. For example:

- **G** Personal guarantee
- **L** Letter of credit

C Colaterral

R Unusually good relationship with Accounts Payable clerks

Form subsection: Date/Last Action

"Most sections of an *Accounts Aging Form* are designed to feed information to management. This section goes beyond information feeding, into information feedback.

"This section gives us feedback on the collection process. Here, we list what collection actions have been taken and when they were completed. When we review this information, we keep several questions in mind.

"Are the A/R clerks following up on accounts? Are they doing it on a timely basis? What collection actions are they taking? Are these actions effective? Are clerks following our prescribed collection timetable/procedures?

"What you find in a column like this may surprise you. For example, you may discover that more clients pay after a collect telephone call than after a letter. If that's the case, you want to make collect calls earlier in the collection cycle.

You may find that clerks avoid making collection calls, because they feel uncomfortable. If that's the case, they need some basic bolstering."

Form subsection: Percentage

"We added percentage columns to our form for two reasons.

"First, it reminded us that Credit and Collections is an aggregate issue. You may have to write off an individual account now and then, but it's not the end of the world. You have to risk money to make money. You have to see the forest for the trees.

"Second, it provides a fast and easy measure of improvement. If the percentages change significantly, we look behind the figures to see what's happening—or, in the case of collections, what's NOT happening!"

SUMMARY

Billing processes and Accounts Receivable control systems are important to a successful C&C program. One generates money, the other penetrates problems. Give them their due by doing the best you can to see that they are designed efficiently and used effectively.

SIMPLE SAMPLE ACCOUNT RECORD

Customer: John Doe
1 Way
Payup, OR 97000

Account #: 007

Date	**Transaction**	**Change**	**Running Total**
1/1	Purchase	+100.00	100.00
1/5	Payment discount	–2.00	
	Payment	–98.00	0.00
1/10	Purchase	+200.00	200.00
2/10	Interest charge	3.00	203.00
2/12	Payment	–200.00	
	Reversal of Interest	–3.00	0.00
	approved by CEO		
2/15	Purchase	+100.00	100.00
2/20	Merchandise returned	–80.00	20.00
	(20% restocking)		
	NOTE: Customer's credit limit doubled to $500		
2/25	Payment	–20.00	0.00

SAMPLE ACCOUNTS AGING REPORT

Client	Total Due	90-120 Days Past Due	60-89 Days Past Due	30-59 Days Past Due	Current
Due-tiful Dyes	5000	3000	2000		
Sing the Blues Dues	4000	2000	2000		
Cray-owe-us	3000		1500	1500	
In the Pen Inc.	3000		1000	1000	1000
Terchniduller Debts	5000		500	500	4000
COLUMN TOTALS	20,000	5000	7000	3000	5000
%	100%	25%	35%	15%	25%

ASK YOURSELF

- What two things must all successful billing and collection systems do? Does yours?
- What are the six major questions that every billing statement must answer?
- What eight design tricks can you employ to make your billing statement more powerful, more motivational?
- What two design tricks can you employ on your billing and/or remittance envelopes to increase their effectiveness?
- At what two levels must accounts be controlled?
- What critical information should appear on every customer account card?
- What should you be able to see on and learn from an Accounts Aging report?

CHAPTER
SEVEN

COLLECTING PAST DUES

THE VANISHING DOLLAR

Step right up folks. Witness the Incredible Disappearing Dollar!

Remember the buck that *Redink Inc.* has owed for the past thirty days? Well, the Commercial Law League of America says that, based on average account collectability, it is worth only 94 cents today! Figure in inflation, and the dollar picture dims even further. Is that amazing?

And wait, there is more. When that business bill is two months past due, its *collectible* worth is a mere 85 cents. At three months, six months, nine months, twelve months and two years past due, it will be worth only 74 cents, 58 cents, 43 cents, 27 cents and 14 cents, respectively.

That is some vanishing act, and it is just the beginning. As the dollar disappears, your profits disappear as well. It is no illusion. The Incredible Disappearing Dollar/Vanishing Profit Act will happen to your ledger if your C&C department is a do-nothing domain.

Considering the relative importance that many small businesses place on Collections, you might be wondering why this book has only one chapter on the subject. Well, any *one chapter wondering* would be the result of a major misperception. All of the chapters in this book are related to collections. By pragmatically practicing the earlier advice in this text, you will be able to avoid most major collection problems. As they say, your best offense is a good defense. The more defensive your credit program, the less offensive you will have to be about collections.

FOCUS ON CREDIT PREVENTION

So when it comes to collections, the most important thing to remember is this: an ounce of Credit prevention is worth a pound of Collection cures. Focus more effort on the first half of the C&C equation, and you will not see so many secondary problems.

Focus the *third half* of your attention on hindsight analysis. When a bad apple slips through your credit granting process, figure out what core problem, or problems, was responsible for the oversight. For example:

- Did you need more financial information on the applicant?

- Did you grant too much credit, too soon?
- Did you rely too heavily on references?
- Did you have faith when you should have had your doubts—or at least you should have had some additional financial guarantees?

Other important rules of thumb can help you win your collection conflicts hands down:

Elements of a Collection Program

There is no one-size-fits-all-businesses *Best Collection Program.* There is only the collection program that works best for you and your business. What works best for you and yours will be a function of:

You

If you hate making collection calls in person, do not make formal field trips part of your collection route. Why? Human nature—if you hate them, you will procrastinate in making them.

You will avoid following up on your collection program. You will decide that it is more important to make sales, make plans, make contacts, make another cup of coffee—you will make any excuse to avoid making The Visit.

Your collection program will fail, not because you cannot do it, but because you will not pursue it. When you design a collection program, make sure that it reflects, rather than rejects, your basic personality, likes and dislikes. If it does not take your abilities and sensibilities into account, it is a no account, no-win program. You will fight your collections program as much as your debtors do.

Your Business Specifics

If you are basically a one-man show, a labor-intensive collections program will not help you show a profit. In fact, it could be such a financial and physical drain that it forces you to close the show down—shortly after the first act.

Your collections program must be a realistic extension of your business. Therefore, it must be a function of your business' wants (e.g., do you want your program to be assertive or aggressive?), needs (e.g., do you need the money by noon or just sometime soon?), personality (e.g., are you basically a pit bull or a lap dog?), abilities (e.g., what and how much can you afford to do?), etc.

Your business is more than a mere organization. It is more like an organism—a living, breathing entity. Do not start a collections program that your business cannot bear to finish. It will finish you both off.

Industry Parameters

If your industry readily accepts ninety-day past due accounts, you had better accept the fact—and these two, too:

- Your best bet for fast payments is a deep discount on C.O.D. and pre- or pretty fast payments. Realistically, in terms of payment dates, your net has been set at three months.
- Collection efforts prior to the generally accepted ninety-day deadline may be viewed by customers, and competitors alike, as pushy, panicky and powerfully unpopular.

Generally, when you go against the industrial grain, you run the risk of reaping tons of animosity.

Acceptable Tradeoffs

Tradeoffs are eminently important in the collection business. For example:

- In your business, collection phone calls may have proven to be more effective than collection letters. However, they may also place additional work and stress on you. Does your monetary gain outweigh this additional strain?
- If you are getting nowhere in dealing with a no-pay purchaser, you could turn his account over to the Due Unto Others Collection Agency. The company's commission would be a cool 30 to 35 percent. Is this such a hot idea?

- Imagine you have a client who owes you $1,000, take or leave $100 in interest charges. If you dropped the interest charges, he would probably pay today. Would it be in your best interest to wait, or to negotiate?

Customer Specifics

Some customers simply pay when they pay. Nothing you do or say to them can or will sway, defray or purvey—absolutely nothing.

Your collections program needs to take this into account. For example, if you deal with government guys, do not push for payment. Just see what you can do to prod the paperwork. No other collection efforts are needed. Governments do pay e-v-e-n-t-u-a-l-l-y.

If a customer does not pay until he receives his first collection letter, make sure that it is sent immediately after his initial billing statement. Why put off until tomorrow what you can do for your dues today?

Recognize and accept your customers and their payment practices for what they are. Do not fight the inevitable—it only costs you money. Know your customers, then design a collections program that you know will meet them and, if necessary, defeat them on their own terms.

Your Turn

Analyze your collection program.

- Is it a comfortable fit relative to:
  - You
  - Your business specifics
  - Your industry parameters
  - Acceptable tradeoffs
  - Customer specifics
- What could you do to improve the fit or leverage your current successes?

THE COLLECTION CONTACT

There is only one major goal appropriate for a collection contact. As a typical businessperson, you may choose one of the following options as the major goal of your dunning letters/calls:

- Prompt a payment
- Come to a settlement
- Resolve a conflict or disagreement
- Stress the importance of early payments
- Remind the customer that he or she agreed to pay the bill within your payment terms
- Inform the customer that unless he or she pays the bill, you will call in his or her personal guarantee—or call in a collection agency, lawyer, etc.
- Make a not-so-subtle threat

If you so choose, *you will loose*. None of the above objectives is acceptable as the major thrust of a collection contact. Absolutely every collection contact should have as its primary goal *establishing communication with the debtor.*

Do not put the cart—the message—before the horse sense—the approach. Think about it. If you do not get through to the debtor, your threat will not be threatening. Your conflict will go unresolved. Your pleas for payment will not please anybody. Clearly, your primary goal is to establish communication. Only then can you establish yourself and your message in the debtor's mind.

IF YOUR METHOD OF CONTACT IS INITIALLY UNPLEASANT, YOU WILL NOT GET THROUGH TO THE DEBTOR. HE WILL CUT YOU OFF AND IGNORE YOUR MESSAGE—PERIOD.

Attitude is Everything

If attitude is critical to the Credit component of the equation, it is hypercritical to the Collections column.

The reason is obvious. People like credit calls because they are predictably positive ("We are giving/extending/increasing credit"). Conversely, collection contacts are necessarily negative ("You owe us . . .").

In addition, most collection contacts are unnecessarily rude, aggressive and/or sarcastic. Collection crews often go overboard in their effort due to personal personnel problems. As noted in Chapter 1, making collection contacts can generate negative feelings such as fear, anger and resentment. Crazed collectors who need to vent their frustrations often do it on their debtors.

The problem: if a client does not want to be your frustration vent, it is easy for him to prevent meaningful contact. For example, you can send a collection letter, but he does not have to read it. You can send a telegram, he does not have to heed it. You can place a collection call, but his secretary or phone facilitator can intercept or interrupt it.

Your Turn

Analyze your last six collection contacts.

- Were you able to maintain a positive collection attitude?

Compile a list of ten things you could have done that would have helped you maintain that positive profile.

If you want to get your foot in the door, you must have both feet planted firmly on the right attitude. No matter what means or media you use to remit your message, you must emit a positive presence. You need to be:

Assertive

There is a mental place about halfway between aggression and apathy, and that is where your head needs to be. If you are too aggressive, too pushy ("Pay up or else . . .") your debtors will push back ("Make me!"). If you are too apathetic, too passive ("Can you please tell me when you're going to pay?"), debtors will pass your bill by ("When we darned well please").

If your attitude is assertive—that is, forthright and forthcoming—you can psychologically *force* debtors into listening to you. Professional people will listen to a professional presentation.

Direct

Be direct about all the relevant who, what, when, where, why and how issues.

Some of the *issues* are not at issue. You know who you wish to address. You know when the items were purchased and when the corresponding debts incurred. You know where the items were shipped.

What you do not know yet, but need to know, is *why* the outstanding bill has not been paid and *how* the debt dilemma is going to be resolved. How do you get the answers to these questions? You ask them.

You must ask clear and unambiguous questions ("Why hasn't this bill been paid?") so that you can get clear and, hopefully, unambiguous answers. If you do not give the debtor direct instructions ("You need to pay *X* dollars by the fifteenth of this month"), he will not know what direction to take.

This is not the time for gamesmanship or guesswork. If you do not get accurate answers to the *why* and *how* questions, you will not know what to do.

Every collection contact should contain a direct, no-nonsense statement as to the consequence of debtor inaction (e.g., "If we have not received a check in the amount of $1,500 by the fifteenth of this month, we will turn this account over to the A-B-Seize Collection Agency"). Be as direct with the debtor as you want the debtor to be with you.

Never threaten an action you are unwilling or unable to take. That will destroy your credibility and can get you into legal trouble.

Informed

You need to approach this parameter from two perspectives:

- Knowledge of the account

  Are you sure the account is, as of your contact time, still past due? Have any partial payments been made? If so, how large were they? Is there a rational reason that the account is past due (e.g., the client will not pay Exterminators Inc. in full until all of the bugs are out of his system)? Has the client talked to anyone else in your firm about his account? If so, what was said and decided?

  BOTTOM LINE: When you talk to the client about his or her past due account, you had better know what you are talking about.

- The client's knowledge of the account

  You know what you know. Does the client? For example, does your client know that his bill is past due? Is he aware that he is being socked 18 percent per annum in interest charges? Does he know that it is your company's policy to refuse additional purchase orders until all three-month-past-due-purchases are paid for? Does he know that your company's policy is to turn all ninety-day past due accounts over to a collection agency? If not, why not?

  BOTTOM LINE: When you finish talking to your client, he or she should know as much about the problem payment's potential problems as you do.

Rational

Your approach should be as cool and rational as possible, considering the fact that somebody has your money and will not give it to you!

Actually, it is that *exclamation point perspective* that gets so many businesspeople in trouble. They forget that it is only money and that they will only get paid if they approach the subject in a rational, businesslike manner.

A rational approach means that you:

- Do not make emotional appeals such as "I have a wife and three children . . ." Collections is not about emotions. It is about your client breaking a legal contract, a formal no-two-ways-about-it payment obligation. Do not weaken your position by addressing your personal weaknesses.

On the other hand, it is a good idea to appeal to your debtor's emotions, as long as you can do it in a rational, reasoned way. Comments like "What would your mother think if she knew you didn't pay your debts"—which appeal to the debtor's conscience—or "I am going to apply to your bank for a loan, and use your past due account balance as collateral"—which prey on his sense of fear—generate emotional baggage, but he ends up carrying it, not you.

- Do not make apologetic or subservient-sounding statements. (For example, "I'm sorry to bother you," "I hate to have to say this" or "I just called . . .".) Never apologize for your collection actions. If there are any apologies to be made, they should come from the debtor. He or she is the one who broke the business bond.

  To avoid having to apologize later for an unwarranted contact, it is wise to hedge your bets. A conditional comment ("Please ignore this note if you have already sent your $1,500 payment" or "According to our records") is all that is necessary.

- Be serious. None of that "You . . . (nervous giggle) . . . owe us money . . . (heh heh) so we would (tee hee) like a check no later than next week . . . (nervous giggle)."

  Having to collect past due accounts is hardly the height of hilarity. It is deadly serious. Writing off a bad debt is not funny business. It is bad business. It can ruin you.

  Laugh all the way to the bank if you want to, but only when you have a check to deposit.

Your Turn

Again, analyze your last six collection contacts.

- Did they establish communication, or did they establish conflict?

- Using your 20/20 hindsight, how could you have enhanced the communication component and lessened the client conflict?

Know Your Customers

By knowing your customers, you know what will motivate them to pay their bills.

Some people respond better to pressure than others. For some, a letter is better than telephone follow up. Some do business with their heads, other with their hearts. Some people are offended if you remind them that their bill is overdue, others are offended if you forget to remind them.

To sum it up: in business, as in life, it takes all kinds.

That is why it takes all kinds of collection approaches. If Customer A likes letters, send A letters. If Business B likes to be phoned, be responsive. If Client C is about to be foreclosed, seize the moment and call your attorney. If Debtor D responds to gladhandling, be glad to give him just that.

In short, do not just do something. Do something that works.

You can leverage Doing The Right Thing by doing the right thing *at the right time.* Most beginning businesspeople devise a set collection cycle: at thirty days past due, we send Letter A; at forty-five days past due, we send Letter B; at sixty days past due, we make Collection Phone Call A or Threat A; at seventy-five days past due, we make Collection Phone Call B or Threat B; at ninety days past due, we tear our hair out.

The common problem with *cyclists* is that they gear up for the long haul system, while stripping their gears in terms of short term opportunities. If, for example, Collection Letters A and B generate virtually no return, while Collection Phone Call A generates reams of remittances, perhaps the company should use the phone call as its first strike, rather than as its third string.

Before Taking Up a Collection

It is wise to consider your return on investment before taking up a collection.

Some collection efforts cost more than others. Using on-site attorneys or collection agencies, for example, is expensive with a capital E. Conversely, generic collection letters are inexpensively true to form. You have to compare the cost—including time, effort and angst involved in a specific collection action—to its potential payback.

Chances are, you want to collect every dollar you have coming to you. Wanting to do that is okay, but deciding to do that is not. You need to put aggregate profits before blind persistence. Collecting money costs money, sometimes *Big Money*. Do not spend $1,000 chasing a $50 debt.

The ugly truth is that in some cases simply writing off a bad debt will hold the most profit potential.

Effective Collection Contacts

Of course, you try to collect using inexpensive letters, phone calls, etc. You do not try the very expensive collection techniques that will cost more money than the payment would generate. Why throw good money after bad?

These general rules of thumb have hands-on value when you start planning your collection contacts. But they are not enough to generate a cost effective *collect effect.* For that, you need to study each individual past due and give it the personal touch.

Before approaching, or reproaching, a past due purchaser, you need to ask yourself three questions:

1. What type of collection contact is most likely to generate a prompt payment?
2. How much would this collection contact cost?
3. If this trade-off between expediency and expense is unacceptably high, is there a form of contact with better promptness or payment payback?

There are four major forms of collection contacts. Each has its own advantages and disadvantages. Fortunately, with a little planning you can promote the pros and constrict the cons:

Collection Letters

There are some pretty persuasive pros relevant to sending collection letters. That is why most businesses use them first when they need to salvage a debt.

The pros of collection letters:

- Inexpensive

  A generic fill-in-the-blanks form letter can be sent to clients for pennies on the debt dollar.

- Fast forwarding

  Sending a form letter to clients takes only minutes.

- Easy to use and automate

  Once designed, form letters are basically clerk work or, to quote one C&C manager, "plodder fodder."

- Easy to edit

  You can work on your form collection letter until it is in perfect form. You need not worry that a comment made in haste will lay to waste your customer or supplier relationship.

- Permanent records of action

  While keeping a record of your efforts will not guarantee a payment in record time, it will make it easy for you to backtrack, and review and analyze the actions you have taken relative to the account.

- Stressless

  Sending a letter, especially a form letter you wrote months ago, is no big deal. That is because receiving a letter, especially a form letter, is no big deal. People deal with paper all of the time. They are paper trained.

Perhaps the con side of the coin is of more importance as a collector's item.

The cons of collection letters:

- Run of the mill

  See *stressless* above. Since they do not generate much interest ("Gee, another collection letter . . ."), they do not generate many payments.

  Debtors do not stop paying their *bill.* They stop paying their *bills*—plural. This means that your collection letter is competing with correspondence from other creditors. If your letter does not stand out, you do not stand a chance of getting paid.

- A one way communiqué

  Communication, by definition, is a two way technique: you give information, you get information. A collection letter assumes that it is easier to give than to receive. In doing so, it gives debtors an easy way out. If they do not want to listen to what you have to say, they can throw your note away.

  WHAT IS WORSE, YOU DO NOT KNOW IF YOUR LETTER WAS READ ON ARRIVAL OR WAS DEAD ON ARRIVAL. If it was not read, it will have no impact—on the debtor or on your Accounts Receivable.

  Collection letters generally generate no feedback. Therefore, they will often heighten, rather than enlighten, your communication problem.

- Without a sense of immediacy

  Collection letters send mixed messages. You tell the debtor that it is important he pay today; yet, your message arrives with a pile of cut-rate catalogs and other inconsequential come-ons. Your letter looks like another piece of personalized junk mail.

  You cannot have it both ways. A mixed message is a nixed message. Your time-sensitive information is corrupted by a delivery that is deficient dramatically.

Increase Your Collection Letter's Effectiveness

If you are going to use collection letters, as virtually all businesses do, you can empower their position by:

- Making them less run of the mill and more of a thrill chill. You can do this in a variety of ways:
  - Make the letter visually appealing. Use high contrast papers and inks. Avoid hard to read glossy papers and small type. Use half sheets for short memos and double wide margins on all memos.
  - Make the letter unique. Use unusual layouts. For example, place the debtor's name and address in the bottom left-hand corner of the letter. Or use an unusual salutation, for example, "Oh, Bob . . .". Or, have your office notary stamp all collections "Correspondence." One successful collections manager gets people to open his letters by drenching their no-return-address-envelopes with expensive perfume. Another successful company includes a lottery ticket ("Don't wait until you win the lottery to pay Invoice # . . .").
  - Make the letter personal. Write your letter in longhand. Do not use metered mail. Highlight or underscore important points with a colored pen.
- Stimulating real communication

  Force and/or facilitate feedback. You can:
  - Create a collections *contract.* Inform the debtor that unless you hear from him by *X* date, you will expect him to follow the deal you have outlined in the letter.
  - Pose a covert threat, overt threat or challenge.

    These comments should not be reserved strictly for collection letters. You can also use them on collection phone calls and on-site visits.

    For example:
    - "Are you going to do *A* or *B*?"
    - "If you don't pay *A* by the fifteenth of the month, you may end up paying *A* plus legal fees, court expenses, etc."

  - "I know you're going to pay someday . . . , and if you do it by the fifteenth you will be able to save your credit."
  - "By contract, we are required to inform our credit bureau of any accounts that are *A* days past due."
  - "I will be forwarding your account to the Shurt, Ofyer, Back and Associates Collection Agency on the fifteenth of the month. You can avoid the complications—and the long term repercussions—of this by sending me your payment right away."
  - Our lawyer wants to know . . ."
- Make it easy for the debtor to contact you. For example, send the debtor two copies of your collection letter. Ask him to write his comments on the back of one copy and return it to you.
- Inform the debtor that you will call him within the week if his payment has not arrived. He will probably call you first.

► Giving the debt status—emergency status.

How do you create collection immediacy? Through image and imagination you can:

► Have your collection letter hand delivered.

► Send your collection letter registered or overnight mail.

► Send your collection letter as a telegram.

CAVEAT: Since telegrams are seen by people other than the recipient, you must word them very carefully. For viable verbiage, contact your local telegram office.

► Stress the date. For example, print the relevant collection date (JULY 15) in letters so big that they cover almost the entire sheet of paper. Provide the particulars in particularly small print ("Pay by this date or we will turn your account over to the Broke 'n Arm Collection Agency").

Collection Phone Calls

The next time you are called upon to make a collection contact, try the telephone; it is on call at all hours. There are even significant advantages to *calling collect.*

The pros of "collect calls":

- Phone calls are inexpensive. You can reach out and touch someone, even put the touch on him for some money, and all it will cost you is a few cents—at least, monetarily speaking. More about that later.
- The phone is fast. Within seconds you can hear the voice of your debtor of choice.

  The telephone's emphasis on immediate action will generate an immediate reaction—hopefully, in the form of a check. If not, at least you get the debtor's immediate response to your stimulus ("I'm not going to pay because . . ." or "I'll pay as soon as you . . .").
- Phone calls are effective. You know when you get through to the debtor ("Is this Francis in Accounting?") and when you do not ("It's that lousy answering machine again!" or "He's still out of the office?"). You know you have had your say, even if you have not gotten your way.
- Phone calls are personal—person-to-person personal. There is no such thing as a form phone call. The people-provided permutations are too prevalent. The debtor needs to respond to what you say, and you need to respond in kind, if not kindly.

The cons of "collect calls":

That is not to say that telephone collection calls are without problems. In fact, they ring in with some major disadvantages:

- Phone calls leave no paper trail. When all is said and done, you cannot prove what was done and said. If, for example, a debtor agrees verbally to settle his account, you have nothing but a verbal agreement—hot air from a not-so-hot customer.
- Collection calls are risky.
  - "Live" collection contacts cannot be changed or refined. What has been said cannot be unsaid.
  - It is difficult to control and manage a telephone call. The debtor may take control of the conversation. He may hang up the phone or not take your call at all.

- Collection calls are *expensive*. Collection calls are cheap moneywise, but expensive otherwise. They exact a high toll in stress ("What if the debtor yells at me or calls me names? What if he's threatening? What if he claims that he's paid?") and procrastination ("He's not there today, so I'll call tomorrow"). These are costs that many collectors are unwilling to pay.

Fortunately, Dialing for Dollars does not have to be a disaster. If you choose to use telephone collection calls, the following tips will help you call the shots:

- Create a paper trail for your phone forays. You should:
  - Keep meticulous notes. Note every who, what, when, where, why and how.
  - Have a second party listen on the line.
  - Send a follow up letter, a pseudo transcript, after all phone collection calls. Summarize what was said and what was promised. Ask the debtor to note any disagreements he may have with your written account.
- Keep control of the conversation by preparing and referring to scripts or checklists. Do not let your debtor devise deliberate discussion detours. Follow your plan (e.g.,"I need to say *X, Y, Z*"). You will make all of your points with pinpoint accuracy.
- Refuse to focus on fears. Stay stressless. Use the *so what* strategy: What is the worst thing that can happen during a phone collection call?
  - The debtor could get rude, crude and lewd. So what?
  - The debtor could get mad. So what? He cannot hit you; all he can do is take his best verbal pot shot.
  - The debtor could take his business elsewhere. So what? If he does not pay his bills, it does not pay to have him for a customer.

On-site Visits

On-site collection contacts are often right on target, particularly when the past due is very old or very large. Pulling into the client's parking lot is a good way to show that you are pulling out all the collection stops.

The pros of an on-site visit

On-site visits offer collectors a visibly different set of advantages than those proffered by collection letters or telephone calls:

- On-site visits are impressive. The mountain goes to Mohammed, so to speak.
- On-site visits cannot be ignored. Debtors can throw away a collection letter or throw up phone-call obstacles ("I don't want you to put through any phone calls from . . ."). They probably will not physically evict you from their businesses.
- On-site visits often generate the fastest payback ("Why don't you cut me a check while I'm here?"). There is no mail lag, no way for debtors to drag their feet.
- On site visits let you do more than focus on one past due bill. They give you an opportunity to network with the purchaser's employees (e.g., people who can help you fast-track future payments). They also provide eyesight into the client's condition ("I see that the client is woefully understocked—perhaps he is in worse financial straits than I had thought. From now on, his purchases are C.O.D.—Cash Or Do without!").

The cons of an on-site visit

Unfortunately, visiting a debtor's place of business is not always good business. On-site collection calls have several major drawbacks:

- On-site collections are very expensive in time, money, aggravation and stress. They are often as hard on the creditor as on the debtor.
- On-site collections are not at all effective if the debtor is out of the office for the day. Chances are that he will not make an appointment with you.

Most businesspeople, however, find that they can make on-site collections without going too far out on a limb. They:

- Check their credit application forms, noting the time(s) that the debtor indicated he would be available via his office telephone. Visit at these times and sometimes he will see you.
- Delegate the collection call to a less-suspicious somebody— namely, the salesperson ("He was able to get the sale, let's see if he's able to get the check!").
- See their on-site visit as a chance to settle the dilemma once and for all. Maybe they will collect the debt, maybe the debt will collect dust. Either way, ending the ignorance is bliss.

Attorneys and Collection Agencies

Attorneys and collection agencies are best used when you have reached a point of no return—that is, you have made your point to the debtor again and again, but there has been no financial return. It is time to give someone else a shot at the debtor. Hopefully, they will have better aim.

The pros of using attorneys/collection agencies

Attorneys and collection agencies can successfully hone in on collection targets. Their advantages:

- Attorneys and collection agencies are collection professionals. They have the networks, contacts, legal knowledge, reputations, etc., necessary to prod payments.
- Attorneys and collection agencies take the ball and run with it. That is, they take the ball, the stress and the effort, away from you. You drop all collection responsibilities, and their related costs. You are free to pursue other business balls.
- Most attorneys and collection agencies take as their fee a percentage of what they take in. If they do not collect the debt, they do not collect from you. A low success rate equals low costs.

The cons of using attorneys/collection agencies

Using attorneys and collection agencies, however, can have an astronomical cost. They will cost you:

- Clients

  Would you continue to do business with someone who sent your business to a collection agency?

  This *cost* is really a *savings.* If going to a collection agency costs you customers, the ones who do not pay their bills, you will save money in the long run.

- Money

  The traditional *take* for attorneys and collection agencies is 30 to 35 percent. This leaves no room for profits or anything else.

Actually, you can negotiate low attorney and/or collection agency costs by:

- Developing and maintaining a good credit program
- Turning accounts over to the attorney and/or collection agency when they are relatively new (forty to sixty days past due)
- Providing your attorney and/or collection agency with an exclusive collection contract

You and the attorney/collection agency should agree to forego the exclusive arrangement when the debtor is outside your geographic area. Local pressure works best.

The above measures decrease the attorney and collection agency's collection costs while increasing their odds of success. Because you are providing *profitable problems,* you can negotiate far-better fees. Some collection agencies will go as low as five percent on long term, high quality business.

MAKING IT WORK

There is no way around it. If you want your Credit and Collection program—particularly the collection component—to work, you have to work at making it work. It all boils down to three words:

Perseverance

Perseverance

Perseverance

Do not give up on a collection.* Charge that interest. Send those invoices. Make those telephone calls. Write those letters. Make those threats. Consult your attorney or contact a collection agency. Work, work, work.

Do what it takes to collect. Then, do it again. And keep doing it. Don't forget the formula for success—which applies more to collections than to any other entrepreneurial activity: success means getting up one more time than you fall down!

* As long as you do not forget to be cost-conscious! Do not spend $15 chasing a $2 debt.

SUMMARY

A collection program is not a collection pogrom. It is an objective, one-debtor-at-a-time, measured response to a serious stimulus.

Actually, your responses need to be more than measured. They need to be immeasurably positive. They need to be communication oriented. They need to be assertive, direct, rational, informed, serious and cost effective. They need to be customized to your personal needs as well as to the wants, needs and expectations of your business, your industry and your customers. Your responses do not need to be all things to all people—they just need to be all of the above things.

The client-specific collection plan only needs to be all things to one person—the debtor. You will need to choose the collection contact—letter, phone call, on-site visit, attorney or collection agency—that you think offers the greatest likelihood of success with the lowest possible cost.

Then, once you decide what you want to do, *just do it.* The road to bankruptcy is paved with pebbles of procrastination.

ASK YOURSELF

- Why is it important to collect past due payments *now*?
- What, relative to collections, is the most important thing to remember?
- Successful collection programs will be a function of what five factors?
- What is the one major goal for all collection contacts?
- What are the four components of a successful collection attitude?
- What is the importance of Return On Investment to your collection efforts?
- What are the advantages and disadvantages of using form collection letters? How can you emphasize the positive and de-emphasize the negative?
- What are the major advantages and disadvantages of personalized collection letters? How can you leverage the good and eliminate the bad?
- What are the major benefits and drawbacks of collection phone calls? How can you promote the pluses and minimize the minuses?
- What are the major pros and cons of on-site visits? How can you enhance the pros and lance the cons?
- What are the major advantages and disadvantages of using attorney and/or collection agencies? What can you do to maximize their value?

RESEARCH SOURCES

RESEARCH SOURCES

There is an old saying: you get what you pay for. Well, if you have ever paid state taxes, you can get your money's worth by using state agencies to answer your questions relative to credit and collection legalities, state/local economic conditions, and your customers commercial/corporate condition.

The cost: nothing. The benefits: invaluable!

List below are the four best state-run sources of C&C, economic and customer information (NOTE: in some states, a single department may provide several of the aforementioned functions). Use the state listings on the following pages to identify the appropriate contact(s) in your area:

- Commerce Corporate Records Office—or the equivalent—for information relative to a customer's commercial background (e.g., is the business a single proprietorship, partnership, corporation? Who is the agent of register/major stockholder?)
- State District Attorney's Office—or the equivalent—for information relative to local C&C rulings/precedents (e.g., is it OK to do such-and-such in this state, in an effort to collect past due accounts?)
- State Economic Development Office—or the equivalent—for information on current economic/demographic conditions and future trends (e.g., is credit in our area getting harder to get? Will our area be growing? Can we get a state grant to purchase credit insurance?)
- Secretary of State's Office—or the equivalent—for information on any Uniform Commercial Code variations that apply in your state

ALABAMA

Corporate Records Dept.
Corporate Division
Office of Secretary of State
Room 524, State Office Building
Montgomery, AL 36130
(205) 261-5326

Attorney General
11 S. Union St.
Montgomery, AL 36130
(502) 261-7400

Department of Economic and
Community Affairs
3465 Norman Bridge Rd.
Montgomery, AL 36105
(205) 284-8706

Secretary of State
State Capitol
Montgomery, AL 36130
(205) 261-3124

ALASKA

Corporate Section
Commerce and Economic
Development Department
PO Box D
Juneau, AK 99811
(907) 465-2530

Attorney General
Department of Law
PO Box K
Juneau, AK 99811
(907) 465-3600

Alaska Industrial Development
Authority
Commerce and Economic
Development Dept.
1577 C St., Suite 304
Anchorage, AK 99501
(907) 274-1651

Lt. Governor
PO Box AA
Juneau, AK 99811
(907) 465-3520

ARIZONA

Incorporating Division Corporation
Commission
1200 W. Washington
Phoenix, AZ 85007
(602) 255-3521

Attorney General
1275 W. Washington
Phoenix, AZ 85007
(602) 255-4266

Department of Commerce
1700 W. Washington, 4th Fl.
Phoenix, AZ 85007
(602) 255-3521

Secretary Of State
Department of State
1700 W. Washington
Phoenix, AZ 85007
(602) 255-4285

ARKANSAS

Corporations Supervisor
Office of Secretary of State
2nd Fl., State Capitol
Little Rock, AR 72201
(501) 371-5156

Attorney General
201 E. Markham Street, Suite 510
Little Rock, AR 72201
(501) 371-2007

Industrial Development Commission
#1 Commerce Mall, RGGm 4-C-300
Little Rock, AR 72201
(501) 371-1121

Secretary of State
262 State Capitol
Little Rock, AR 72201
(501) 371-1010

CALIFORNIA

Corporate Filing Division
Office of Secretary of State
1230 J Street
Sacramento, CA 95814
(916) 324-1485

Attorney General
Department of Justice
1515 K. St., Suite 511
Sacramento, CA 95814
(916) 324-5347

Department of Commerce
1121 L. St., Suite 600
Sacramento, CA 95814
(916) 322-3962

Secretary of State
1230 J. Street
Sacramento, CA 95814
(916) 445-6371

COLORADO

Division of Commercial Recordings
Department of State
1560 Broadway, Suite 200
Denver, CO 80203
(303) 866-2311

Attorney General
Department of Law
1525 Sherman St., 3rd Fl.
Denver, CO 80203
303) 866-3611

Department of Local Affairs
13213 Sherman St., Room 518
Denver, CO 80203
(303) 866-2771

Secretary of State
Department of State
1560 Broadway, Suite 200
Denver, CO 80203
(303) 866-2762

DELAWARE

Corporate Division
Department of State
Townsend Building
Dover, DE 19901
(302) 736-3073

Attorney General
Carvel State Office Building
820 N. French St.
Wilmington, DE 19801
(302) 571-2500

Development Office
99 Kings Highway
Dover, DE 19901
(302) 736-4271

Secretary of State
Department of State
Townsend Building
Dover, DE 19901
(302) 736-4111

FLORIDA

Devision of Corporations
Department of State
The Capitol
Tallahassee, FL 32301
(904) 487-6900

Attorney General
Department of Legal Affairs
The Capitol
Tallahassee, FL 32301
(904) 487-1963

Division of Economic Development
Department of Commerce
510-C. Collins Building
Tallahassee, FL 32399-2000
(904) 488-6300

Secretary of State
The Capitol
Tallahassee, FL 32301
(904) 488-3680

GEORGIA

Corporations Division
Office of Secretary of State
2 Martin Luther King Jr. Dr., SE
3rd Fl, W. Tower
Atlanta, GA 30334
(4C4) 656-2806

Attorney General
State Law Department
132 State Judicial Building
Atlanta, GA 30332
(404) 656-4585

Department of Industry and Trade
230 Peachtree St., N.W.
Atlanta, GA 30301
(404) 656-3556

Secretary of State
214 State Capitol
Atlanta, GA 30334
(404) 656-2881

HAWAII

Department of Commerce and
Consumer Affairs
1010 Richards St.
Honolulu, HI 96813
(808) 548-7505

Attorney General
State Capitol
Honolulu, HI 96813
(808) 548-4740

Department of Business and
Economic Develpoment
250 S. King St.
Honolulu, HI 96813
(808) 548-6914

Lt. Governor
5th Fl., State Capitol
Honolulu, HI 96813
(808) 548-2544

IDAHO

Secretary of State
Statehouse
Boise, ID 83720
(208) 334-2300

Attorney General
Office of the Attorney General
Statehouse
Boise, ID 83720
(208) 334-2400

Department of Commerce
Statehouse
Boise, ID 83720
(208) 334-2470

Secretary of State
Statehouse
Boise, ID 83720
(208) 334-2300

ILLINOIS

Director of Corporations
Office of Secretary of State
328 Centennial Building
Springfield, IL 62756
(217) 872-1835

Attorney General
500 S. Second St.
Springfield, IL 6270
(217) 782-1090

Department of Commerce and
Community Affairs
620 E. Adams St., 3rd Fl.
Springfield, IL 62701
(217) 785-1032

Secretary of State
213 State House
Springfield, IL 62706
(217) 782-2201

INDIANA

Corporation Section
Office of Secretary of State
155 State House
Indianapolis, IN 46204
(317) 232-6578

Attorney General
219 State House
Indianapolis, IN 46204
(317) 232-6201

Industrial Development
Department of Commerce
One N. Capitol, Suite 700
Indianapolis, IN 46204
(317) 232-8888

Secretary of State
201 State House
Indianapolis, IN 46204
(317) 232-6531

IOWA

Corporations Director
Office of Secretary of State
2nd Fl., Hoover Building
Des Moines, IA 50319
(515) 281-5204

Attorney General
Hoover State Office Building
Des Moines, IA 50319
(515) 281-8373

Department of Economic Development
200 E. Grand
Des Moines, IA 50309
(515) 281-5571

Secretary of State
201 State House
Indianapolis, IA 46204
(317) 232-6531

KANSAS

Secretary of State
2nd Fl., State House
Topeka, KS 66612
(913) 296-2236

Attorney General
Judicial Center
Topeka, KS 66612
(913) 296-2215

Secretary
Department of Economic Development
503 Kansas Ave., 6th Fl.
Topeka, KS 66603
(913) 926-3480

Secretary of State
2nd Fl., State House
Topeka, KS 66612
(913) 296-2236

KENTUCKY

Secretary of the Commonwealth
State Capitol Building
Frankfort, KY 40601
(502) 564-3490

Attorney General
State Capitol
Frankfort, KY 40601
(502) 564-7600

Economc Development
Department Commerce Cabinet
Capitol Plaza Tower
Frankfort, KY 40601
(502) 564-7670

Secretary of the Commonwealth
State Capitol Building
Frankfort, KY 40601
(502) 564-3490

LOUISIANA

Secretary of State
Department of State
PO Box 94125
Baton Rouge, LA 70804
(504) 342-5710

Attorney General
Department of Justice
PO Box 94005
Baton Rouge, LA 70804
(504) 342-7013

Secretary
Department of Commerce
PO Box 94185
Baton Rouge, LA 70804
(504 342-5388

Secretary of State
Department of State
PO Box 94125
Baton Rouge, LA 70804
(504) 342-5710

MAINE

Deputy Secretary of State
Bureau of Corporations
State House Station #101
Augusta, ME 04333
(207) 289-3501

Attorney General
Department of the Attorney General
State House Station #6
Augusta, ME 04333
(207) 289-3661

Director State Development
Office Executive Department
State House Station #59
Augusta, ME 04333
(207) 289-2656

Secretary of State
State Department
State House Station #101
Augusta, ME 04333
(207) 289-3638

MARYLAND

Department of Assessments and
Taxation
301 W Preston St.
Room 806
Baltimore, MD 21201
(301) 225-1184

Attorney General
Seven N. Calvert St.
Baltimore, MD 21202
(301) 576-6300

Industrial Financing Authority
Economic and Community
Development Department
2244 World Trade Center
Baltimore, MD 21202
(301) 659-4263

Secretary of State
26 Francis St.
Jeffrey Building
Annapolis, MD 21401
(301) 974-3421

MASSACHUSETTS

Secretary of the Commonwealth
Room 337, State House
Boston, MA 02133
(617) 727-2800

Attorney General
One Ashburton Pl.
Boston, MA 02108
(617) 727-3688

Governor's Office of Economic
Development
Room 109, State House
Boston, MA 02133

MICHIGAN

Corporations and Securities Bureau
PO Box 30222
Lansing, MI 48909
(517) 334-6212

Attorney General
525 W. Ottawa, Law Building
Lansing, MI 48913
(517) 373-1110

Michigan Division
Department of Commerce
PO Box 30225
Lansing, MI 48909
(517) 373-3550

Secretary of State
1st Fl, Treasury Building
Lansing, MI 48918
(517) 373-2510

MINNESOTA

Corporations Division
Office of Secretary of State
180 State Office Building
St. Paul, MN 55155
(612) 296-2803

Attorney General
102 State Capitol
St. Paul, MN 55155
(612) 297-4272

Economic Development Division
Department of Energy and Economic
Development
150 E. Kellogg Blvd, Room 980
St. Paul, MN 55101
(612) 296-2976

Secretary of State
180 State Office Building
St. Paul, MN 55155
(612) 296-2079

MISSISSIPPI

Corporations Division
Office of Secretary of State
401 Mississippi St.
Jackson, MS 39201
(601) 359-1350

Attorney General
5th Fl, Gartin Building
Jackson, MS 39201
(601) 359-3680

Department of Economic Development
1201 Sillers Building
Jackson, MS 39201
(601) 359-3449

Secretary of State
401 Mississippi St.
Jackson, MS 39201
(601) 359-1350

MISSOURI

Director of Corporations
Office of Secretary of State
Truman Building
PO Box 778
Jefferson City, MO 65102
(314) 751-4194

Attorney General
Supreme Court Building
PO Box 899
Jefferson City, MO 65102
(314) 751-3221

Department of Economic Development
PO Box 1157
Jefferson City, MO 65102
(314) 751-4962

Secretary of State
Room 209, State Capitol
PO Box 778
Jefferson City, MO 65102
(314) 751-4195

MONTANA

Corporations Bureau
Office of Secretary of State
State Capitol
Helena, MT 59620
(406) 444-3665

Attorney General
Department of Justice
215 N. Sanders St.
Helena, MT 59620
(406) 444-2026

Business Assistance Division
Department of Commerce
1424 Ninth Ave.
Helena, MT 59620
(406) 444-3923

Secretary of State
Room 202, State Capitol
Helena, MT 59620
(406) 444-2034

NEBRASKA

Secretary of State
Room 2300, State Capitol
PO Box 94608
Lincoln, NE 68509
(402) 471-2554

Attorney General
Room 2115, State Capitol
PO Box 94906
Lincoln, NE 68509
(402) 471-2682

Department of Economic Development
301 Centennial Mall A.
PO Box 94666
Lincoln, NE 68509
(402) 471-3111

NEVADA

Secretary of State
State Capitol
Carson City, NV 89710
(702) 885-5203

Attorney General
Heroes Memorial Building
Capitol Complex
Carson City, NV 89710
(702) 885-4170

Commissioner on Economic
Development
600 E. William, Suite 203
Carson City, NV 89710
(702) 885-4325

NEW HAMPSHIRE

Secretary of State
204 State House
Concord, NH 03301
(603) 271-3242

Attorney General
208 State House Annex
235 Capitol St.
Concord, NH 03301
(603) 271-3658

Department of Resources and
Economic Development
PO Box 856
Concord, NJ 03301
(603) 271-2341

NEW JERSEY

Divison of Commercial Recordings
Department of State
State House, CN 300
Trenton, NJ 08625
(609) 984-6412

Attorney General
Department of Law and Public Safety
Justice Hughes Complex, CN 080
Trenton, NJ 08625
(609) 292-4976

Division of Economic Development
Commerce and Economic
Development Department
One W. State St., CN 823
Trenton, NJ 08625
(609) 292-7757

Secretary of State
Department of State
State House
Trenton, NJ 0862
(609) 984-1900

NEW MEXICO

Corporations Division
Corporation Commission
PO Drawer 1269
Sante Fe, NM 87504
(505) 827-4508

Attorney General
Bataan Memorial Building
PO Box 1508
Sante Fe, NM 87501
(505) 827-6000

Cabinet Secretary
Department of Economic Development
and Tourism
1100 St. Francis Dr.
Santa Fe, NM 87501
(505) 827-6204

Secretary of State
State Capitol
Santa Fe, NM 87503
(505) 827-3601

NEW YORK

Secretary of State
Department of State
162 Washington Ave.
Albany, NY 12231
(518) 474-4750

Attorney General
Department of Law State Capitol
Albany, NY 12224
(518) 474-7330

Chairman and President
Urban Development Corp
One Commerce Plaza
New York, NY 10036
(212) 930-0200

NORTH CAROLINA

Corporations Attorney
Corporations Division
Office of Secretary of State
300 N. Salisbury St.
Raleigh, NC 27611
(919) 733-4201

Attorney General
Department of Justice
Justice Building, Box 629
Raleigh, NC 27602
(919) 733-3377

Industrial Development Division
Department of Commerce
430 N. Salisbury St.
Raleigh, NC 27611
(919) 733-4151

Secretary of State
State Capitol
Capitol Square
Raleigh, NC 27611
(919) 733-3433

NORTH DAKOTA

Corporations Division
Office of Secretary of State
1st Fl., State Capitol
Bismarck, ND 58505
(701) 224-3669

Attorney General
1st Fl, State Capitol
Bismarck, ND 58505
(701) 224-2210

Economic Development Commission
Liberty Memorial Building
State Capitol Grounds
Bismarck, ND 58505
(701) 224-2810

OHIO

Director of Corporations
Office of Secretary of State
30 E. Broad St.
Columbus, OH 43215
(614) 466-8464

Attorney General
30 E. Broad St., 17th Fl.
Columbus, OH 43266
(614) 466-3376

Division of Business Development
Department of Development
30 E. Broad St.
Columbus, OH 43266
(416) 466-2317

OKLAHOMA

Secretary of State
101 State Capitol
Oklahoma City, OK 73105
(405) 521-3911

Attorney General
112 State Capitol
Oklahoma City, OK 73105
(405) 521-3921

OREGON

Corporation Division
Department of Commerce
158 12t. St. N.E.
Salem, OR 97310
(503) 378-4383

Attorney General
Department of Justice
100 State Office Building
Salem, OR 97310
(503) 387-6002

Business Development
Department of Economic Development
595 Cottage St., N.E.
Salem, OR 97310
(503) 373-1240

Secretary of State
136 State Capitol
Salem, OR 97310
(503) 378-4139

PENNSYLVANIA

Corporation Bureau
Department of State
308 N. Office Building
Harrisburg, PA 17120
(717) 787-1379

Attorney General
Strawberry Square, 16th Fl.
Harrisburg, PA 17120
(717) 787-3391

Department of Commerce
43 Forum Building
Harrisburg, PA 17120
(717) 787-3003

Secretary of State
Department of State
302 N. Office Building
Harrisburg, PA 17120
(717) 787-7630

RHODE ISLAND

Director of Corporations
Corporate Division
Office of Secretary of State
Smith St.
Providence, RI 02903
(401) 277-3040

Attorney Genera
72 Pine Street
Providence, RI 02903
(401) 274-4400

Department of Economic Development
7 Jackson Walkway
Providence, RI 02903
(401) 277-2601

Secretary of State
State House
Providence, RI 02903
(401) 277-2357

SOUTH CAROLINA

Secretary of State
PO Box 11350
Wade Hampton Building
Columbia, SC 29211
(803) 734-2155

Attorney General
Dennis Building
PO Box 11549
Columbia, SC 29211
(803) 734-3970

State Development Road
1301 Gervais Street
PO Box 927
Columbia, SC 29202
(803) 734-1400

SOUTH DAKOTA

Secretary of State
2nd Fl., State Capitol
Pierre, SD 57501
(605) 773-3537

Attorney General
3rd Fl., State Capitol
Pierre, SD 57501
(605) 773-3215

Governor's Office of Economic Development
Capitol Lake Plaza
Pierre, SD 57501
(605) 773-5032

TENNESSEE

Division of Corporations
Office of Secretary of State
5th Fl., James K. Polk Building
Nashville, TN 37219
(615) 741-2286

Attorney General
450 James Robertson Parkway
Nashville, TN 37219
(615) 741-6474

Department of Economic and Community Development
32 Sixth Ave.,
N. Nashville, TN 37219
(615) 741-1888

Secretary of State
State Capitol
Nashville, TN 37219
(615) 741-2816

TEXAS

Corporate Division
Office of Secretary of State
Box 13697 Capitol Station
Austin, TX 78711
(512) 463-5586

Attorney General
Box 12548 Capitol Station
Austin, TX 87811
(512) 463-2100

Economic Development Commission
Box 12728 Capitol Station
Austin, TX 78711
(512) 472-5059

Secretary of State
Box 12887
Capitol Station
Austin, TX 78711
(512) 463-5701

UTAH

Division of Corporations
Department of Business Regulation
160 E. 300 St.
Salt Lake City, UT 84111
(801) 530-6016

Attorney General
236 State Capitol
Salt Lake City, UT 84114
(801) 533-7661

Division of Business and Economic Development
6150 State Office Building
Salt Lake City, UT 84114
(801) 533-5325

Lt. Governor
203 State Capitol
Salt Lake City, UT 84114
(801) 533-5111

VERMONT

Corporations Division
Office of Secretary of State
26 Terrace St.
Montpelier, VT 05602
(802) 828-2386

Attorney General
Pavilion Office Building
109 State St.
Montpelier, VT 05602
(802) 828-3171

Department of Development
Agency of Development and Community Affairs
109 State St.
Montpelier, VT 05602
(802) 929-3221

Secretary of State
Redstone Building
26 Terrace St.
Montpelier, VT 05602
(802) 828-2363

VIRGINIA

State Corporation Commission
13th Fl., Jefferson Building
Richmond, VA 23219
(804) 786-3604

Attorney General
Office of the Attorney General
101 N. Eigth St., 5th Fl.
Richmond, VA 23219
(804) 786-2071

Department of Economic Development
1000 Washington Building
Richmond, VA 23219
(804) 786-3791

Secretary of the Commonwealth
Office of the Secretary of the Commonwealth
Room 112, Ninth St. Office Building
Richmond, VA 23219
(804) 786-2441

WASHINGTON

Corporate Division
Office of Secretary of State
505 E. Union, M/S PM-21
Olympia, WA 98504
(206) 753-7120

Attorney General
Office of the Attorney General
Temple of Justice
Olympia, WA 98504
(206) 753-2550

Domestic and International Plant/Facility Development
312 First Ave. N.
Seattle, WA 98109
(206) 464-6282

Secretary of State
Legislative Building
Olympia, WA 98504
(206) 753-7121

WEST VIRGINIA

Secretary of State
State Capitol
Charleston, WV 25305
(304) 345-4000

Attorney General
Room E-26, State Capitol
Charleston, WV 25305
(304) 348-2021

Governor s Office of Community and International Development
State Capitol Complex
Charleston, WV 25305
(304) 340-0400

WISCONSIN

Corporations Division
Office of Secretary of State
PO Box 7846
Madison, WI 53707
(608) 266-3590

Attorney General
Department of Justice
114 E. State Capitol
PO Box 7857
Madison, WI 53707
(608) 266-1221

Bureau of Business Expansion and Recruitment
Department of Development
114 E. State Capitol
PO Box 5970
Madison, WI 53702
(608) 266-1605

Secretary of State
201 E. Washington Ave., Room 271
Madison, WI 53702
(608) 266-5801

WYOMING

Corporations Division
Office of Secretary of State
State Capitol
Cheyenne, WY 82002

Attorney General
State Capitol
Cheyenne, WY 82002

Economic Development and Stabilization Board
Herschler Building
Cheyenne, WY 82002
(307) 777-7287

Secretary of State
State Capitol
Cheyenne, WY 82002
(307) 777-7378

DISTRICT OF COLUMBIA

Corporations Division
Department of Consumer and
Regulatory Affairs
614 H. St., N.W., Room 407
Washington, D.C. 20001

Corporate Counsel
Office of Corporation Counsel
1350 Pennsylvania, N.W., Room 329
Washington, D.C. 20004
(202) 727-6248

Economic Development
1350 Pennsylvania, N.W.
Washington, D.C. 20004
(202) 727-6600

Secretary of the District
District Building, Room 521
1350 Pennsylvania, N.W.
Washington, D.C. 20004
(202) 727-6306

MORE ABOUT THE NATIONAL ASSOCIATION OF CREDIT MANAGERS

The National Association of Credit Managers is a national association that has local affiliations throughout the U.S. These local liaisons can help you with a number of substantial benefits, including:

- Sample forms
- C&C "environmental" research
- Informational pamphlets, newsletters, magazines and books
- Credit/legal updates (local, national, and international)
- Lobbying leverage
- Professional training and seminars
- Professional certification
- Credit reports (local, national and international)
- Fraud information (general fraud profiles, specific fraud practitioners, etc.)
- Collection services (local, national and international)
- Invaluable advice

For your nearest NACM affiliate:

ALABAMA
Birmingham 205-591-5300

ARIZONA
Phoenix 602-252-8866

CALIFORNIA
Los Angeles 213-381-2661
1-800-541-2622
San Diego 619-239-8191
San Francisco 415-351-7500

COLORADO
Denver 303-837-1280

CONNECTICUT
Bridgeport 203-659-2666
Hartford 203-659-2666
New Haven 203-659-2666

D.C.
Washington 703-65S-7900

FLORIDA
Orlando 305-299-7491
Tampa 813-877-9457

GEORGIA
Atlanta 404-491-3313

HAWAII
Honolulu 808-536-3741

ILLINOIS
Chicago 312-696-3000

INDIANA
Evansville 812-425-2651
Indianapolis 317-632-4444

IOWA
Cedar Rapids 319-364-2463
Des Moines 515-279-2232
Waterloo 319-266-5141

KANSAS
Wichita 316-263-1257

KENTUCKY
Louisville 502-583-4471

LOUISIANA
New Orleans 504-523-1701

MARYLAND
Baltimore

MASSACHUSETTS
Boston 617-648-4500

MICHIGAN
Detroit 313-827-1280
Grand Rapids 616-459-3371
Lansing 517-332-8426
Muskegon 616-722-3711

MINNESOTA
Minneapolis 612-341-9600

MISSOURI
Kansas City 816-931-7115
St Louis 314-842-0056

MONTANA
Billings 406-652-3454

NEBRASKA
Omaha 403-2480

NEVADA
Reno 702-323-6167

NEW JERSEY
Red Bank 201-842-4141

NEW MEXICO
Albuquerque 505-889-7717

NEW YORK
Binghamton 607-563-9411
Buffalo 716-854-7018
New York 212-741-2266
Rochester 716-654-9100
Syracuse 315-675-3506

NORTH CAROLINA
Charlotte 704-333-1254

NORTH DAKOTA
Fargo 701-293-8282

OHIO
Akron 216-384-1717
Cincinnati 513-241-3841
Cleveland 216-357-1200
Dayton 513-288-6124
Mansfield 419-884-l012
Toledo 419-476-4426
Youngstown 216-746-0607

OKLAHOMA

Oklahoma City 405-235-1341

OREGON

Portland 503-226-3531

PENNSYLVANIA

Philadelphia 215-923-1765

Pittsburgh 412-344-1400

RHODE ISLAND

Providence 401-727-1300

TENNESSEE

Knoxville 615-546-0452

Memphis 901-726-4505

Nashville 615-248-5890

TEXAS

Amarillo 806-358-3184

Dallas 214-637-3753

El Paso 915-593-2300

Fort Worth 817-457-7912

Houston 713-523-3341

Lubbock 806-744-2359

Odessa 214-637-3753

San Antonio 512-225-7106

UTAH

Salt Lake City 801-487-8781

VIRGINIA

Norfolk 804-436-3604

Richmond 804-353-2711

WASHINGTON

Seattle 206-728-6333

Spokane 509-326-2550

WISCONSIN

Madison 608-271-7500

Wilwaukee 414-258-1800

ABOUT THE AUTHOR

Lynn Harrison is a consultant, author and professional speaker who has written 14 books and over 150 articles on business issues such as credits and collections, taxes and employee productivity. Ms. Harrison has also appeared on CNN, SNN and "The Today Show," and was profiled in the *New York Times, Woman's Day,* and the *Saturday Evening Post.*

NOTES

NOTES

NOTES

NOTES

NOTES

NOTES

ABOUT CRISP PUBLICATIONS

We hope that you enjoyed this book. If so, we have good news for you. This title is only one in the library of Crisp's best-selling books. Each of our books is easy to use and is obtainable at a very reasonable price.

Books are available from your distributor. A free catalog is available upon request from Crisp Publications, Inc., 1200 Hamilton Court, Menlo Park, California 94025. Phone: (415) 323-6100; Fax: (415) 323-5800.

Books are organized by general subject area.

Computer Series

Beginning DOS for Nontechnical Business Users	212-7
Beginning Lotus 1-2-3 for Nontechnical Business Users	213-5
Beginning Excel for Nontechnical Business Users	215-1
DOS for WordPerfect Users	216-X
WordPerfect Styles Made Easy	217-8
WordPerfect Sorting Made Easy	218-6
Getting Creative with Newsletters in WordPerfect	219-4
Beginning WordPerfect 5.1 for Nontechnical Business Users	214-3

Management Training

Building a Total Quality Culture	176-7
Desktop Design	001-9
Ethics in Business	69-6
Formatting Letters and Memos	130-9
From Technician to Supervisor	194-5
Goals and Goal Setting	183-X
Increasing Employee Productivity	010-8
Introduction to Microcomputers	087-6
Leadership Skills for Women	62-9
Managing for Commitment	099-X
Managing Organizational Change	80-7
Motivating at Work	201-1
Quality at Work	72-6
Systematic Problem Solving and Decision Making	63-2
Twenty-First Century Leader	191-0

Personal Improvement

Business Etiquette and Professionalism	032-9
Managing Upward	131-7
Successful Self-Management	26-2
Americans With Disabilities Act	209-7
Guide to OSHA	180-5
Men and Women—Partners at Work	009-4

Communications

Better Business Writing	25-4
Technical Writing in the Corporate World	004-3
Writing Business Reports and Proposals	122-8

Small Business and Financial Planning

The Accounting Cycle	146-5
The Basics of Budgeting	134-1
Credits and Collections	080-9
Financial Analysis: The Next Step	132-5
Personal Financial Fitness	205-4
Starting Your New Business	144-9
Understanding Financial Statements	22-1
Writing and Implementing a Marketing Plan	083-3